ANATOMY OF THE VIRGIN BIRTH

EMMANUEL ELENDU

Copyright © 2017 by Emmanuel Elendu

Anatomy of the Virgin Birth
By Emmanuel Elendu

Printed in the United States of America

ISBN: 10: 0996459006
ISBN: 13: 978-0-9964590-0-6

All rights reserved. No part of this book may be reproduced, stored in retrieval system, or transmitted in any form or by any means: electronic, mechanical, photocopies, recording, scanning or other-except for brief quotations in critical reviews or articles, without the prior written permission of the publisher. This book or parts thereof may not be reproduced in any form, stored in a retrieval system, or transmitted in any form by any means - electronic, mechanical, photocopy, recording, or otherwise without prior written permission of the publisher, except as provided by the United States of America copyright law. Unless otherwise noted, all Scripture quotations are from the New King James version of the Bible. Copyright © 1979, 1980, 1982 by Thomas Nelson, Inc., publishers Used by permission.

Cover Design By: Faith Walley

Published By:
Cibunet Publishing
P. O. Box 444
Woodlawn, NY 10470
Email: admin@cibunet.com
Website: www.cibunet.com

TABLE OF CONTENTS

DEDICATION..4

FOREWORD..5&7

INTRODUCTION...14

RISING FROM OBSCURITY............................18

Chapter One
THE HOLY SPIRIT..27

Chapter Two
MARY...51

Chapter Three
JOSEPH...71

Chapter Four
THE WISE MEN...91

Chapter Five
HEROD..109

REFERENCES...155

DEDICATION

To the children in my life, biological and spiritual; and especially to

Samuel, David and Ruth

FOREWORD

There is a unique assignment for everyone on earth. Though we may all desire to pursue what brings fulfillment and gratification, the reality is that many of us become so saddled with so much human, systemic and demonic opposition that we quit on divine destiny prematurely.

It is hard to convince a lot of people that they have a destiny designed by God to bring them to the place of fulfillment. Others who may accept this reality still wonder if God made the right choice in view of their apparent dysfunctions and displacements. Those who lay their hands to the plow and may have started taking steps in pursuit of divine purpose sometimes abandon the path of divine destiny when the barriers and limitations become too overwhelming. With Satan actively working to distract and derail those who set their hearts to follow after God's plan for their lives, it is essential that we develop our insights into how God intends for us to emerge as overcomers.

The scriptures are full of historical accounts of people who played a role in God's redemptive plan to save mankind from the consequences of Adam's fall. Notable is the story of the birth of Jesus Christ the Son of God, who was sent by the Father into this earth to become the sacrifice for our sins.

There are several books that explain to us the process of salvation and deliverance from bondage but not many authors have undertaken to capture the revelation behind the virgin conception. The story of Mary and Joseph who were engaged but yet to become a married couple, as well as the wise men and Herod, all underscore the dynamics of how God works through people to accomplish great things in the face of opposition.

The role of the Holy Spirit in the incubation of dreams, visions and prophetic revelation by believers and the schemes of the kingdom of darkness to apprehend divine agenda is articulated in such a vivid way that equips the reader to emerge victorious over the enemy.

Throughout the book, Pastor Elendu uses simple illustrations and testimonies that not only inform, but equips the reader to build a solid personal relationship with the Holy Spirit. I trust that you will have a deeper encounter and experience greater victories through the manifold revelations enshrined in this book.

Dr. Kenneth Walley
President of KWI and New Faith Tabernacle Churches.

FOREWORD

*By
Dr. Obiwu Iwuanyanwu
Anatomy of the Virgin Birth ... (Spiritual Tourism
and the Struggle for Redemption)*

Pastor Emmanuel Elendu's Anatomy of the Virgin Birth reminds me of another religious book that I had come across many years ago, "Be Not Afraid!" (1984), by Pope John Paul II. As in "Be Not Afraid!," Anatomy of the Virgin Birth is about trust, faith, and courage. Both books especially help us to explore the unique path of Christian spiritual discovery as a personal, individual journey. Like the Pope, Elendu presents the search for God through his son Jesus Christ as a quest that turns our world upside down and conquers the mystery of fear. But Elendu goes even further.

Anatomy of the Virgin Birth is probably the first book I have read, apart from the Bible itself, which closely deals with the significations of the principal characters and personalities that surround the person of Christ himself. Many of us would know (especially those of us who are Roman Catholics) that there are Three Persons in One God. Pastor Elendu's interpellative tool, however, confronts this reading and carries it further to broaden our understanding of the personas of The Holy Spirit, Mary, Joseph, The Wise Men, and Herod.

In other words, Anatomy of the Virgin Birth is a book that enjoins us to take a second look at the old question of who is the Holy Spirit and revaluate his relationship to the Child Jesus and God the Father. The book makes us to reexamine our knowledge of Mary Mother of God and her relationship to the other Marys of the New Testament. Elendu pointedly confronts the question of who is Joseph the Carpenter, and what is so special about such lowly and ordinary folk as Mary and Joseph that they are found worthy of such world-changing responsibilities as becoming the mother and the father of the most high, the son of God? He breaks down the façade that is Herod and the failing game he devices for the manipulation of the three wise men.

More than anything, Anatomy of the Virgin Birth is a book by a man of God who doubles as a spiritual or religious tourist. One thing that will be obvious to every reader of this book is that the author has been to the Holy Land of Israel and knows the nooks and dimensions of such iconic locales as Bethlehem and Jerusalem. The reader is, therefore, often led by imaginative leaps to scour the contours of the hills and homes, vales and vines that mark the breath and feet of Christ. Pastor Elendu is a well-traveled and vastly knowledgeable preacher whose writing lifts the sensory immediacy of his environment with the urgency of his message.

The title would, of course, echo Chinweizu's masculinist, anti-feminist Anatomy of Female Power (1990), but it doesn't go any further than that veneer connection. Whereas Chinweizu's book represents the capitalist, if opulent, materiality of women and the female body, Elendu's Anatomy of the Virgin Birth represents the purity and immateriality of the female body. In a sense, Pastor Elendu could have been aware of the earlier book and therefore, consciously or unconsciously, set out to write a counter-narrative that seeks to preserve the integrity of the woman as a spiritual being, one who would rise above the grass and mundane violability of Chinweiu's ideological commodification.

What is never lost to the reader, ultimately, is that Anatomy of the Virgin Birth is the story of physically challenged and impoverished people who choose, and are therefore chosen, to present themselves as vessels of God's triumphant battle over adversity and death. In this connection the book shares the focal thrust of a popular Nigerian Igbo grade school song, "Uwa Bu Ndoli, Ndoli." As the song goes:

The song is a clarion call for a life that defies defeatism, in the same vein that Pastor Elendu's book offers Christians a view into a life that eschews mortality through the defiance of the risen Christ. On the one hand, Anatomy of the Virgin Birth is a book that asks women (as would-be mothers) and men (as would-be fathers) to prepare themselves as instruments, change agents, and revolutionaries of God on earth. On the other hand, it is a book for every reader who wants to enjoy good writing and, at the same time, learn something of the unique story of the mystery of Christ as Man and God.

References
Chinweizu. Anatomy of Female Power: A Masculinist Dissection of Matriarchy. Lagos: Pero Press, 1990.
John Paul, Pope, and Andre Frossard. "Be Not Afraid!": John Paul II Speaks Out on His Life, His Beliefs, and His Inspiring Vision for Humanity. New York: St Martin's Press, 1984.

Dr. Obiwu Iwuanyanwu, Ph.D. (Syracuse), is an associate professor of English and creative writing at Central State University, Wilberforce, Ohio. He is the author of four books, including Rituals of the Sun (poetry), Tigress at Full Moon (poetry), Igbos of Northern Nigeria (Diaspora studies), and The Critical Imagination in African Literature (critical theory).

pages 124-130
Schemes of men in Civil Society

1. What is there for me in this scheme?
2. I must make money by whatever and any means possible
3. My political stand is defined by what gets me elected into office
4. Life is about what you get out of people, program or projects; the denominator is the dollar
5. There is no absolute in ethics or morals in business; the end justifies the means
6. I must get what I want, when I want it and how I want it. I have no obligations to anyone
7. Success is seen in what you have, who you are and where fame and acclaim have met you
8. I am the boss; whatever I say stands in this office. You are an employee under my payroll
I don't care about values and beliefs. Man is what he makes or does not make for himself.
Everything depends on what you can handle. God is an euphemism. Hell and heaven are here on earth

A new wave of values in the Church
1. I am redeemed to be rich, blessed to be happy. That is what I am created for.
2. Anointing without money translates to annoyance in ministry.
3. I must make it (money) in ministry by force or by fire; my God is not a poor God.
4. Our Church is known for mass production of men known for their wits and grits for material possession

5. Truth is really subjective, there is no absolute. Bible is only a guide, not the whole truth. Jesus is not the only way to God.
6. Whatever religion you belong, all God wants from you is to be a good person

A good Church is known for its programs, music, shows, outdoor activities and community involvement

I am called to make men rich (financially) and appeal to emotions and psyche so that people do not get hurt again

We love people to the point that we cannot begin to insist on a certain way to live (choices) or dictate who their spouses are; there is no such thing as man or woman, just address them as 'significant other' or 'spouses'

The Holy Spirit is an influence, a staged drama and belongs to the Bible times, not now.

The fight for supremacy in the Family (Home)
1. Everybody has equal rights and privileges in this home
2. My thing belongs to me, there is no trespassing. I have my space, you have yours
3. I am so proud of my job and profession. Nothing comes in between, not even my family
4. My husband (wife) is such a terrible person. I will give him (her) a death certificate; wouldn't stop at a divorce document

5. I am in this marriage for what I gain out of it, remember, I am the King's kid

6. I took a vow: 'for better, for richer; in wealth and in happiness; forever happy and blessed" I stand by this.

7. I thought I was going to change her (him), she (he) is like every other lady (man) on the street

8. I am not going to have babies (my pets can suffice) because I have only one life to live and must enjoy it to the maximum

9. I do not have to disclose everything to my spouse, some secrets may be necessary against the rainy day

10. Respect and love are reciprocal outcomes. She respects me, I will love her. He loves and provides for me, I will offer my body to him.

INTRODUCTION

Some 400 years behind time, Isaiah declared that a virgin shall bring forth a Son in Bethlehem of Judea, the city of David. Among critics of the virgin birth this is laughable, especially when one observes and runs through Bethlehem: a restive, elevated, and mountain-circled city in Central Israel. Bethlehem is not a hub for commerce as you find in Joppa (Tel Aviv), or Haifa, or Azotus (Ashdod), or Gaza. It is not a political fulcrum of the Palestinian natives. It does not make headline news, or has almost everything running the course of 'business as usual' and taking its cues from the big cities of its time. Bethlehem is just one of those cities with a normal life. Bethlehem lies five miles south by west of Jerusalem, a little to the east of the road to Hebron. It occupies part of the summit and sides of a narrow limestone ridge which shoots out eastward from the central chains of the Judea mountains and breaks down abruptly into deep valleys on the north, south, and east. Its old name, Ephrath, meant "the fruitful." Bethlehem means "house of bread." Its modern name, Beitlaham, means "house of meat." It was the home of Boaz and Ruth, of Jesse and David. The modern town contains between five hundred to one thousand houses, occupied by Greek-church Christians. Over the rock-hewn cave which monks point out as the stable where Christ was born, there stands a church built by the Empress Helena, A. D. 325-327, which is the oldest monument to Christ known to men. Bethlehem was a suitable birthplace for a spiritual king, as suitable as Rome would have been a temporal king. As we drove towards this hill countryside, it resonated in me that this was where my Lord was born. The serene, calm welcome from the circling hills, the imposing trees as though imported from Lebanon, the peace in the air (except for armed teens and fortified soldiers on guard) tell you that Bethlehem is indeed a place where the most important birth, in the history of humanity, took place.

As we consider the Anatomy of the Virgin Birth, it is the intention of this piece of prose to assume that the subject of Virgin Birth is a belief you strongly hold and live with; and so, I do not intend to go into apologetics nor theological treatise or some debates that have previously held in higher fora. The aim of this piece to highlight the roles of the characters we identified in the story of the birth of our Lord Jesus Christ. Insight into the Roles of:

1. The Holy Spirit
2. Mary
3. Joseph
4. Three wise men
5. Herod

From a Pentecostal and Evangelical point of view, I will be treating these subjects with the hope that the Lord will bless your life as we apply lessons learned and power given from above. The whole idea is to see a Church living its dreams and a people energized to take back power and authority in the Kingdom of our Lord, as replicated on Earth.

> Dearest of all the names above,
> My Jesus, and my God,
> Who can resist Thy heavenly love,
> Or trifle with Thy blood?
>
> "Tis by the merits of Thy death
> The Father smiles again;
> "Tis by Thine interceding breath
> The Spirit dwells with men.
>
> Till God in human flesh I see,
> My thoughts no comfort find;
> The Holy, Just, and Sacred Three
> Are terrors to my mind.
>
> But if Emmanuel's face appear,
> My hope, my joy begins;
> His name forbids my slavish fear,
> His grace removes my sins.
>
> While Jews on their own law rely,

And Greeks of wisdom boast,
I love the incarnate mystery,
And there I fix my trust.

RISING FROM OBSCURITY

At the call of times, Jesus Christ could be imagined as one born to a poor carpenter, his claim and engagements were a foray of things hoped for by the agonizing Israeli nation. He could have well been crowned King of the Jews, fulfilling the yearnings and clamor for deliverance from Roman torture and years of occupation in the East and West Bank. Here was a Son who it was imagined, would bring hope and succor; a Son who the nation depended on, to emancipate and reinstate the pride that was once called "God's people" brought into limelight from obscurity; a nation that was called by God "to occupy and possess a land overflowing with milk and honey ... a land that was shown to the patriarch, Abraham." This was inheritance by fiat, by decree. Suddenly things changed. First it was Egypt that took the stage. Egypt plundered the inheritance and made slaves out of a people called by the Governor of nations.

Through the passage of time, it became obvious that this small group of people would pass through the corridors of power and hate, in the hands of its neighbors, friends, and foes to form a nation which was once foretold its ancestors. Josephus and other Jewish historians advanced the scripting of events around and within Israel's ordeal and emergence from hate, envy, and torture. As these stories unfold, there arose a glare of hope for the very few who cared to take notice of history and had desired for deliverance. This emancipation from slavery and sin was expected. Rome was in full gear to cut to size on any dissident who would defy the ruling class or cast a spell on Caesar. Power must be preserved. Resources from the people must also flow into the treasury, at least to keep the wheel of industry rolling. Money was a major factor in the play of power; the end that justified the means. So with all the set order and governance, it was certain that men were pushed to the wall. The zealots on one hand were diehard Pharisees who would not tolerate Rome's unwelcome insurgence. They had grown wary with the preaching 'according to the law' and were almost 'giving up' on when a Deliverer would emerge. Soon another group, the militants (or the anti-government, anti-Roman crusaders) could not tame their patience any longer. They would occasionally organize riots and disrupt governance, almost always making the annexed State of Israel ungovernable for Caesar and his governors. Barnabas was one of such 'rebel' leaders. To Israel, he was a true son, a deliverer, and a just man; to Rome he was a rebel; so, depending on who you ask on the street, Barnabas was a personality of mixed grill. In the midst of all these, there echoed, again, that a Savior, a Deliverer was born.

The world of Israel must have gone agog with such news. The ecstasy and glamor; the relief and burden lifting such antecedence brought hope after these long years of waiting. Aha! God can again visit with a Deliverer! To me, Israel was not mistaken to fix all her hope on this one last slice of pizza that must quench the hunger for deliverance for many years. You may wonder why the constant and continuous gaze at a tiny country called Israel. Why the unleash of terror and hate? Why the occupation and slavery from Egypt, the Assyrians, the Hittites, Moabites, and all those Iraqis, Iranians, and all that? You wonder, after all, these nations are richer in resources (courtesy of God-given petroleum products and precious stones). They have large land mass and an exquisite number of gifted men (talking about the Greeks) and warlords like the Romans. Why the hate and the insurgence on a tiny small nation? Simple: I find out that when God speaks concerning a man or a nation, when He makes a declaration over a life, the Earth and its inhabitants with all the assigned demons in their secret locales set themselves to work. They energize their tactics to undoing the Spoken Word of prophecy. Their inertia to undo and kill a vision is maximized until they declare "mission accomplished" And so it is with Israel. God spoke to Abraham: "I will bless thee and thy seed ... I will make thee a father of many nations ... Isaac, not Ishmael, shall be the heir." Since that time, Israel has been under the siege of the enemy. A ploy to exterminate and wipe the nation out of world map has been the primary waking thoughts of many nations who hate God and what He stands for.

Concerning Jesus Christ, the Scriptures Attest in Isaiah 7:1-14. **"Therefore the Lord Himself shall give you a sign; Behold, a virgin shall conceive, and bear a Son, and shall call His name Immanuel."** This Immanuel shall be the Deliverer. The style and similitude of this Deliverer was not made public but the power and authority were laid bare by the prophets.

Here is Isaiah again (9: 6&7 KJV), **"For unto us a Child is born, Unto us a Son is given; And the government will be upon His shoulder. And His name will be called Wonderful, Counselor, Mighty God, Everlasting Father, Prince of Peace. Of the increase of His government and peace, There will be no end, Upon the throne of David and over His kingdom, To order it and establish it with judgment and justice, From that time forward, even forever. The zeal of the Lord of hosts will perform this."**

Considering all these, every Israeli must be certain that a King will come to deliver them from oppression. Therefore when the time was ripe, John the Baptist started from where Malachi stopped, to prophesy and charge on the people to prepare for the coming of this King. It was certain that hell was let loose. To the best of my knowledge, there was an agitation within forces of darkness because they knew their times and days were numbered. They knew the Son would soon be revealed who will come to take possession of his Father's inheritance and reinstate Man in his original position. They knew that judgment was on its way.

Out of obscurity, in the dark ends of Bethlehem (a city of David) of Judea, a virgin was spotted. All these we will learn together as we continue in this book. But permit me to mention; out of obscurity you may have purchased this book. It may also be that a word has been spoken about you by God: that a star is born. You may have been inclined to a dark passage of time; your moments have been chalked with fleeting phases of ephemerals; your center cannot hold any more. There is hope for you. You will find life in Jesus Christ as you read of His birth; indeed, your rebirth. At Jesus' weaning in the temple, Simeon declared: **"For my eyes have seen your salvation, which you have prepared in the sight of all nations: a light for revelation to the Gentiles, and the glory of your people Israel."**

The child's father and mother marveled at what was said about him. Then Simeon blessed them and said to Mary, his mother: **"This child is destined to cause the falling and rising of many in Israel, and to be a sign that will be spoken against, so that the** thoughts of many hearts will be revealed. And a sword will pierce your own soul too" (Luke 2:30-35 KJV).

Your eyes shall see the salvation of God! As it was with Jesus so it shall be for you because He has gone up to the Father (on behalf of you) and "all things are ours." There is hope for you. There is life, an everlasting life awaiting! You will rise from obscurity! Permit me to share a letter that Ron Walters (Senior Vice President of Ministry Relations, Salem Communications) wrote me a few months ago. He permitted the reprint here. Ron writes:

"Good morning,
The United States Military Academy, class of 1915, was dubbed, "The class the stars fell on." The moniker was given because 59 of the 164 graduates eventually became generals in the United States Army. With so many up-and-comers to choose from, who would have guessed that the most decorated of them all would be the one labeled as average?

Leadership is a funny game; stardom wears a mysterious cloak. Greatness doesn't come from physical stature, or by barking orders in booming decibels. Otherwise, General Dwight D. Eisenhower would have been just another soldier. The road to the top, in his case, came through the quiet halls of the servants' quarters. Young Eisenhower—called "Ike" from early childhood—was a poor farmer's kid from Kansas. He entered the military only because West Point offered him a tuition-free education. And although he possessed a brilliant mind, it rarely translated into noticeable achievements. Ike ranked 61st academically, and 125th in discipline among his West Point graduates. He was therefore branded as average—good enough to be commissioned a second lieutenant, but not much else. He applied for an overseas assignment, but was denied. Instead, he was assigned the obscure stateside position of staff officer. Then, for sixteen years, he plateaued at the rank of major. His talents were locked inside his quiet demeanor and diminutive frame.

Even during the Second World War, Ike held a desk job in Washington D.C. for the first year of the war. He garnered no headlines, raised no eyebrows. Little was expected from this bright but placid man. How he moved from his desk job, leapfrogging 366 senior officers, to become commander of U.S. troops in Europe, and then to Supreme Commander of the Allied Forces, is still one of history's great mysteries. But this much we know: the heat of battle has an uncanny way of reinventing a soldier ... or a pastor. Foxholes tend to magnify inner resources, to unveil the real person. Some wilt in battle. Others wait. But leaders jump. Ike jumped. The iconic names of Patton, Bradley, Nimitz and MacArthur all catapulted to hero status during the war. But none ascended to the rarified air as did D.D. Eisenhower. (George Patton, having been passed over in favor of Eisenhower, claimed D.D. stood for Divine Destiny.)

Who could imagine that Eisenhower would be the man to lead history's largest and most successful military machine? Certainly not Winston Churchill who was forever frustrated by Eisenhower's tentative manner. Certainly not Britain's top soldier, General Allen Brooke, who said, "Eisenhower is hopeless. He knows nothing about military matters." Even President Roosevelt, from time to time, second-guessed his choice of commanding general.

But in time it became obvious: the demanding yet like-able Ike was indeed the right man for the job. Even his enemies agreed. Hitler's propaganda minister, in his post-war comments wrote, "The performance of the American Theater Commander had made the playing field uneven." Not bad for an average guy.

Throughout time many surprising and very average candidates have risen to greatness, but none more so than those who were handpicked by God. He has a way of changing the ordinary into extraordinary at the sovereign blink of His eye.

For example:
- Joseph's brothers considered him expendable, but God used him to save a nation from starvation.

- Moses was an 80-year-old shepherd before God gave him the career move of a lifetime.
- Eliab unceremoniously reminded David how insignificant he was ... just before the younger brother taught the Philistines that nobody, including a giant, can taunt God's people and get away with it.
- Peter, the 1st century's foot-in-mouth specialist, became God's keynote speaker on the Day of Pentecost.
- Paul, a cantankerous, disabled hothead, was used by God to write half of the New Testament.

Even Jesus was clothed in average wrappings. As Isaiah said, **"He had no beauty or majesty to attract us to Him, nothing in His appearance that we should desire Him."** God has chosen you to lead his troops, and His choices for leadership rarely fit the corporate mold. It's not about stature or bravado, but humility and tenacity. Attributes that are often considered wholly average to the masses, He counters with exceptional.

Blessings

CHAPTER ONE

THE HOLY SPIRIT

"Now the birth of Jesus Christ was on this wise: When as his mother Mary was espoused to Joseph, before they came together, she was found with child of the Holy Ghost" (Matthew 1:18 KJV)
The Commander in Chief of the heavenly army; the Supreme Architect and Principal Founder of the designs and construction of the heavens and earth; the Maker and Mender of men (with all the physiology and anatomy of every detailed framework of man), expressed in people as a Spirit; but posts as God in the universe and beyond; He is the Holy Spirit. When He visits, naive men call Him a wind; they look for the remains or implants of His impressions by way of miracles. He is more than a miracle worker. In other remote instances, He shows

up as a Guest to a meeting. A visit leaves men dazed and with awe. Some fall under the anointing, others feel an electrifying run through the body, and thus slump under His power. Such men rise empowered and strengthened. They say they have been baptized by the Holy Ghost. He is more than a baptizer.

The doctrine of the virgin birth has been described and accepted as the truth of all generations and ages. The acts, personality, and implants of the Holy Spirit in these end times on humans leave us with much to experience and share. Suffice it to say that this small exposé would capture an infinitesimal content to who the Holy Spirit is and what He does. At the virgin birth, there seems to be a full course operation of this Personality that would benefit the body of Christ. His involvement and style of operation lends itself for scrutiny and thereby an offer to be employed by any reader. The Holy Ghost came on Mary. When, How, Where? Let's find out!

1.1 When the Holy Ghost Comes ...

At the upper room on the 50th day after Jesus Christ ascended into heaven the disciples gathered, praying. That meeting must have been a private caucus put together by a few, joined alongside by certain proselytes (Jewish converts from other nations who came to Jerusalem for some other businesses and religious obligations). Some must have come in fear, not knowing the next state of events surrounding the demise of the One who led a mass revolution and were suddenly cut off. They must have wondered if the risen Jesus, who more than 500 hundred watched ascend into heaven with an evidence of an empty tomb (from His death) would come to restore and deliver Israel from the cruel and inhumane oppression by the Romans, as promised. Downtown, there must be this exciting song of victory by the Pharisees and ruling class that seem to drown any hope that, after all, the Messiah meant what He said when He charged them in response to a question whether He was going to restore the kingdom to Israel. He had replied;

"And he said unto them, It is not for you to know the times or the seasons, which the Father hath put in his own power. But ye shall receive power, after that the Holy Ghost is come upon you: and ye shall be witnesses unto me both in Jerusalem, and in all Judaea, and in Samaria, and unto the uttermost part of the earth" (Acts 1:7&8 KJV)

The folks in the upper room were mere men; men exposed to the realities of life. Men whose leader was killed and there seemed to be an overwhelming state of anxiety, disrepair, and desperation, and wasted years of building a ministry or a revolution in the past three years of following, learning, and want. Some came with the big question, 'What's next?' 'Where do we go from here?' 'What's the next move?' They were mere men like us. In the trial of events and fear of the unknown, in those questions and confusion amidst the prayers, God remembered them. It was time for the Holy Spirit to come. The question as to the validity of the baptism of the Holy Ghost does not invite a debate by motivational speakers to decide. It is unnecessary. The timing and showing are only within the confines and foray of God's schedule. The real issue is in knowing 'when the Holy Ghost comes.' When He comes, He will make all things known. His manifestations will be obvious; the impact will tell the full story.

Amidst your fear, confusion, and desperation God knows where you are and how long you have dwelt on the other side of your life. Mary must have, along with other beautiful girls in her neighborhood and community, been waiting to know who this fortunate mother of the Savior, would be. I suppose Mary, like Daniel, read through the Torah and the Scroll about the coming of the Messiah, and with John the Baptist's declaration that the Deliverer was soon to be revealed. Like Mary, you may be asking, 'When will He come?' 'What is the sign of His influence and occupation?' 'Will God select me among the many virgins of our time, to be a mother to this baby?'

But when the Holy Ghost comes, He will truly come on you. The expectation and wait will be worth the while, because it attests to the need to wait. Big dreams come during deep sleep; when the far ends of the earth are silent; when the noise and commotions on earth have ceased. At such times, there is a whisper, a still small voice pointing to the one true path to greatness. I encourage you to stay the course and keep waiting, keep watching; wait for the time when He comes. The Holy Ghost will surely come.

"Cast not away therefore your confidence, which hath great recompense of reward. For ye have need of patience, that, after ye have done the will of God, ye might receive the promise. For yet a little while, and he that shall come will come, and will not tarry. Now the just shall live by faith: but if any man draw back, my soul shall have no pleasure in him. But we are not of them who draw back unto perdition; but of them that believe to the saving of the soul" (Hebrews 10:35-39 KJV)

1.2 You Will Be Overwhelmed

God does not show up in a life for fun. Like a responsible Father, the advent of the Holy Spirit is for a particular purpose, for specific assignments. When the Holy Ghost comes on you, God intends that He gets on to the assignment He came to do. Like Mary, He came on her to 'plant the seed of God' in her. She was overwhelmed. When the Holy Ghost comes on you, help comes; you are empowered to do extraordinary things. Though He is the General Commanding Officer of the armed forces of heaven, yet He comes into a man as a gentle, soft-spoken, peaceful personality. His roots and genre are of the Father, an epitome of a tranquility that takes a cue from the heavenly serenity and the enduring peace of the Father. Even at that, the Spirit overwhelms the house, His new habitation. You may wonder why Mary asked, "How can I be the mother of my Lord?" The experience of the implantation of the seed of God in a woman tells a story about creation in the garden. Mary was the vessel, the same way molded clay was the vessel. You may want to call it a 'jar of clay.' This clay was to contain the breath of God, the seed of God. As the Lord spoke life into this clay, it became a living soul. We call this soul, man. Mary was a vessel and as God overwhelmed her, implanting His Seed in her, she carried this seed and nurtured the Seed until the day of showing. It is an overwhelming experience for a man to carry a prophetic word from the Lord, to carry a Baptism by Fire and to run with it. Permit me to say that it overwrites imagination to know that mortal man is made to carry His Maker (by way of the Spirit); to carry a vision of an eternal Father; one which transcends his times and seasons. Such was Mary. She was overwhelmed, entirely engulfed by this experience.

As we wait for the descent of the Holy Spirit, may I urge you to expect an overwhelming influence; an experience of a life time. When the Holy Spirit comes, you will be transformed. You will see heaven and it's Christ. Your values will change. Your care-about will be different. There will be a transformation, a change in the things you value most which will result to a change in the way you do things, including ministry. You will be overwhelmed. There will be a swift move from the natural to the supernatural. The Holy Ghost that came upon Mary, the experience of a jar of clay comes alive, that clay never lived like before. Mary was overwhelmed and totally changed. She became drunk with new wine. The transformation the Holy Ghost brings to bear on a man has a truncating but intoxicating effect on the man. Nowhere has the Holy Ghost showed face that He did not leave some impressionable marks on the man. At the upper room, men and women spoke in languages foreign to the native tongues with interpreters standing by. The people accused the disciples of being drunk with new wine in the wee hours of the day. Hannah was accused of Eli on the same account just because the Holy Ghost took over, as she prayed her heart out in search for a son.

At Mahannaim as Jacob journeyed to meet his brother Esau, he sent his two spouses, his two female servants and eleven sons over the ford of Jabbok as he reclined to self and thought of next strategy (He feared Esau was going to attack him because of what he did to Esau). Jacob was left alone. At that moment, he saw a vision and engaged in a nightlong wrestle with the Lord. He needed a change, a blessing. Jacob knew that the power of God was present and he could not prevail over God. God prevailed and left him limping, but he obtained a blessing. His name got changed from Jacob to Israel (Genesis 32:22-32). When a man meets God, there is an impact on his life that leaves a trail of God on him. The Holy Spirit does not come for fun. He is constantly engaged in the business of regeneration, deliverance, and reconciliation. You know something has happened. He leaves a proof of ownership behind for the world to know that there is a repossession of God's property. The man is drunk with wine ... and the world knows it!

1.3 Drunk with wine?

Wait for Him; He will surely come, Wait! (1 Samuel 1:10, 13-16; Acts 2:1-5)

Do you drink liquor? Have you been arrested for Driving Under the Influence of alcohol (DUI)? If you have, then you will understand what I am about to say. As the scripture says, "Give wine to a miserable man so that he can drink and forget his sorrows," is true for a drunkard. Intoxicating drinks are not meant for rulers or those who want to lead a useful life; they are not to be consumed by the clergy or anyone who leads and intends to lead; instead, they serve to quench misery and temporarily pacify the ailing heart. When wine takes control of a man, the man moves and acts based on the whim and power of the wine. The same is true of the Holy Ghost. When a man is under His influence, the man moves and acts under His influence. He is no more in control of himself. The man is occupied by the Holy Ghost. The same was true of Mary. Normally, when a man drinks wine, the influence does not wane until after sometime. For drunks, they keep the tipsy state going (for the love of the influence) and the only way to do that is to keep drinking and engage in certain activities (walking, talking, or dancing). As long as the drunk continues to drink, his nerves and blood agree to an equilibrium level; thus the system gets plateaued to the level the brain can contain; beyond that point, the lever is affected and problems arise; but to keep going, the drunk keeps drinking. I learned something from that: to be drunk with the wine of the Spirit, all I need to do is to get plateaued; to keep drinking; never stopping. To be filled with Holy Spirit is one of the most exciting experiences of a life time. I keep seeking and drinking from the cisterns of the Holy Ghost. He empowers and energizes. He is life and He sustains the man. Mary had a good experience and you too can share from the same. As the Spirit comes, do you imagine His overwhelming influence, being filled with new wine? This wine can sustain a life. It keeps you going, with power and strength. Mary was filled with the Holy Ghost. You too can be filled today! **"Be ye filled not with wine but with the Holy Spirit"** (Ephesians 4:18).

2. There was hunger and thirst in Mary's heart

The Holy Ghost fills a hungry heart; He steps in to fulfill a need. One thing is noteworthy of God, and that is that as much as God wants to fill us and, indeed, fill the whole world with His Spirit, He diligently searches for those who thirst and seek Him. As a manager of useful resource, God does not waste eternal and divine resources on lay abouts, on people who just want to have fun with precious seeds. No, God does not do that. He seeks a useful life. He looks for those whose hearts are sold to making the best use of precious ornaments. He seeks hungry hearts to pour His Spirit in. When He finds such hearts and assures Himself that such a life can be trusted and something precious can be poured inside of it, He goes on to fill the vessel for His glory. Suffice to say that the problem God has today is to find a Mary to pour Himself into. There is scarcity of Marys; a drought of willing vessels in our age. Many Marys have been born in my generation and at birth, there was an echo, a declaration that a vessel was set aside for God to prepare and use. Soon after weaning, there needed to be a raising, an equipping.

But the devil went on rampage. Those Marys lost grip and grit. Their vessels got contaminated and thus discarded. God could not use them again. God's hope seemed dashed against a wall. Too bad! What went wrong? The cares and frivolities of life got into the vessels and wasted precious seeds, at least in the 'use plan' of God.

Mary was betrothed to Joseph, yet she kept herself pure and sanctified. One thing stood out in Mary: she was ready; there was hunger and thirst for an infilling. She was hungry for reality. She lived in anticipation for the coming of the Deliverer. The descent of the Spirit was not without an announcement. That announcement meant that it was not a sudden, magical act. It was clear that a Messiah was coming but many girls knew about it and did nothing to prepare to be filled, to be used by God to bring to life the Baby. Mary knew better. She got her heart ready and God did not neglect such attention to a search for Him.

"**He who seeks me shall find me, and that early,**" says the Lord. It is the search for reality and essence of living. As we wait for the baptism of the Holy Ghost, for the Lord to appear, does it resonate in our hearts to seek Him with a sincere, pure heart? The knowledge that God does little with mediocre and drags, with novices, should compel us to take Him serious when we are about a heavenly assignment. Mary knew that for God to have faith in her there must be some serious search for a sustainable energy that goes against the evil days ahead. There must be a desire to eat to her fill because the journey to carry her God within her womb was not a trivial journey. It had to be taken seriously. And she took it with every seriousness it deserved.

Another thing I find with God is that He seems to ignore a precious life even at moments of despair and scarcity. It seems to me that He chooses to test and try the one He wants to use, to determine the quality product or character that has been formed in the man. Sometimes the enemy leaches out assaults, hell lets loose its tantrums, and it seems God has gone on vacation. You think you will crack and die; not so. God is taking notice. Your soul is precious before His eyes. You will not die! You will find examples of these in the life of God's people. Israel (Exodus 2:13-15) cried under the bondage of her slave masters. Her cry went to God. Again, Israel (Isaiah 7:1-10) was devastated by Assyria and its allies. The same experience happened in the time of Gideon (Judges 6). In all these situations, the people were almost crushed. Mary must have waited with a thirst and desire to be favored. Your wait may have caused you pain, but it is worth the waiting. Are you prepared for the big event in your life? It is an event that only God can perform. The play will soon begin but the question on the lips of the heavenly hosts is,

"Is he ready for the stage?" Or, "Is he still playing the big boy on the gallery of life, picking the crumbs instead of the precious seed, the seed of the word of life?"

3. The brooding influence... and effect

As the Holy Ghost indicates His preparedness to encamp in a mortal man, His urge to do extraordinary things with a mortal man, I believe the design and building stages are set. Even God is involved in the program. He has made all things ready to execute this project. The angel reached out to Mary: **"Hail Mary/ full of grace/ thou art favored among all women."** At this point the decision to be a carrier of the message was left with Mary. She was left with the will power to say yes or no to the message by the angel. Since she had waited and was eager to receive, the delivery was smooth and easy. Mary offered her body to be with the Child as the Holy Ghost came upon her. In our walk with the Lord, He approaches with an offer to fill us with His power and presence. In our hearts, we can either accept or reject His offer to come in, or to overwhelm us, or to empower us. For Mary, hers was a case of 'the Holy Ghost coming over her.' In other words, the Spirit came on; literally brooded over her. How can this be, you seem to ask? The theology and philosophical arguments around this claim are not for us to discuss here, but permit us a little example of how these experiences can be applied in our daily lives as we pay attention to the instructions of the Father.

Example with an egg under mother hen...

Heat is needed to form life in an egg. During incubation (twenty-one days sitting of the mother hen on its fertilized egg) heat is generated and in the process of time, the egg yolk begins to form the chick, the flesh. As more heat is generated, fathers continue to form from the egg white; out of the body and wings. When the chick is formed, mother hen pecks on it to allow the chick to come out. One important factor in the incubation of the egg is the heat generation. Today, technology hastens that process by providing adequate heat environment for the chick to form. Whichever way the egg is incubated, heat is an inevitable factor. It's a wonder how heat incubates an egg into a chick, and this leads me to think about the 'incubation' of Mary by the Holy Ghost. As the Holy Ghost came on Mary, she conceived a Son in fulfillment of the prophecy of Isaiah. Mary again was willing and obedient; submitted herself under the power of the Holy Spirit. Assuming the egg tells the mother hen, "I am not ready now, I want to be alone, I am suspicious of the heat you provide, so please leave me alone." Or the egg simply pulls herself out of the brooding and incubation being provided by mother hen, off the covering mother hen provides, that egg stays outside and rots away. This is what some of us do.

As the Holy Ghost comes, He wants us to come under His influence, to be incubated and infused with life. He appeals to us to come closer to the Father, but we choose a distant worship, to operate from afar off. Since incubation can only take place at a proximity, in which case those afar off cannot benefit from it, this process of life-infusion is stayed. Mary was willing and obedient. She subjected herself to the Holy Ghost, and the Spirit provided the 'heat' and life was formed. The fire of the Spirit is available to anyone who will yield to His call. As He provides heat, life is formed; power is generated and the son in you will begin to manifest. God's intention is not to save us so that we stay at the gallery watching and wishing great things to happen. He wants us to be conduits of miracles, channels of His power. Get up, go, sit under an anointed worship where the Word is preached with power and the Truth is practiced. There ask the Holy Ghost to incubate you; to fill you. When you do that by Faith (serving the Lord), you will catch the fire. There will be a transfer of power. The seed of God planted by the Word inside of you is energized to perform. In other words, God's DNA inside of you begins to blossom. The current begins to flow; there is life formed inside of you. The Holy Spirit is for all to profit and to perform. He has been given to the

Church and you are part of the Church of the living God. The scripture says, **"For out of your belly shall flow rivers of living water."** This is the overflowing of the Holy Spirit.

4. Pregnant with the Holy Ghost (Isaiah 9:6&7) **"Therefore the Lord Himself shall give you a sign; Behold, a virgin shall conceive..."** (Isaiah 7:14)

Behold, just see, a virgin shall conceive ... she shall bear a child ... she is with a child. As the Holy Ghost came on Mary, she conceived and carried her baby in the womb. The same is expected of you: to conceive and carry the Holy Ghost around. Permit me to ask: Are you pregnant with the Holy Ghost? This question is very important in our walk with the Lord Jesus Christ. Man, since after the fall, has been craving for the filling in of the vacuum created by the absence of the Father in fellowship. The void that needs to be filled screams and vents for what would replace or fill it that man readily finds a soothing agent to fill this gap. He gets into different activities including search for money, occult practice, trying out different religions all to no avail. Beyond that he moves into the shopping malls and engages in a buying spree. Man has to satisfy a need to fill a vacuum. He is pregnant with something, something to fill his bowels with and satisfy a longing which God had designed for Himself alone. It is this passion and crave for something that is the point of emphasis here.

Someone was asked this question about God's creation: "What surprised you most about God's creation?" He answered: "MAN!" Because he sacrifices his health to make money; then he sacrifices money to recuperate his health; and then, he is so anxious about the future that he does not enjoy the present; the result being that he does not live in the present or the future; he lives as if he is never going to die; then he dies having never really lived."

What really is your passion?
What are you pregnant with?
What drives you?

Mary was pregnant with the Holy Ghost. Are you pregnant with something bigger than you? Do you have an idea that you will leave for generations unborn? There must be something driving you, something ordained by God for your life. A child should be in your womb by the Holy Spirit. As you prepare to be a career of the Spirit, there could be imminent danger if you do not do the following, but I pray earnestly that you will be equipped to fulfill these demands and be a home for the Spirit of God.

Flush out the old man

By nature man was born in sin and the devil devastated him by reason of inherited sin. Sin reigned in man until Jesus Christ came to redeem him. Sometimes the old man resurfaces and practices his doctrines in man. To be a carrier of the Holy Ghost, one must be emptied of the old man. Self and personal ambition must give way for the new man to blossom. The dominant gene of the old nature comes with all the dirty stuff of envy, ego, selfish accumulation of wanton riches, gossip, lies, arrogance, and many other vices. For the Spirit to fully reside in a man and be fully in charge, He wills that the body be cleaned out. The age long adage that says you cannot put a new wine into an old wine skin becomes imperative in our context. New psyche, new reasoning, new vessel, new Spirit. Mary was a virgin, brand new from the Manufacturer; never contaminated. At new birth, God wants our vessels to stay clean, ready to be filled with the Holy Ghost.

As the Holy Spirit is released, something happens to you. Do not forget that you are getting into a new realm of experience. It is akin to the experience at the Upper Room in Jerusalem when the Lord came as a rushing wind and tongues of fire. The baptism and empowerment can take place at the same time. As the Lord descends, you may speak a language that is foreign to you; you may begin to feel electrified or dazed. Some folks begin to feel a current running through their spines. You are not in control of yourself. At this time, the Lord is saying, 'I am in charge of your life, allow me to work through this mass of clay and empower it for something glorious'. As the Holy Spirit comes on you, you may experience a lifting and the aura of His presence is all you need to receive instructions and power. Pay close attention to what He has to say.

Permit me to share an experience: At what used to be General Hospital in Aba, Nigeria (Abia State University Teaching Hospital), we gathered to pray after a week-long fasting and praying for the salvation of souls in that city. I led the prayer meeting that evening. Over a period of 30 days there had been this charge from a conference we attended (Nigerian Fellowship of Evangelical Students at Zaria, Nigeria), that we were all liable to the souls around us, that we must do everything to save them from destruction and be custodians of the souls who were headed to hell fire. It was a pursuit of righteousness and the business of God. We were all engaged and zealously went about the search for souls. As we sought, we prayed. As we prayed on this fateful Saturday evening, the Holy Ghost came down. The hall was full. Men, women, boys, and girls were dazed, and it was obvious the Lord was with us. I was lifted up off the floor. We were soaked with power, blasting in tongues. The Lord asked me to open my eyes. I did. I saw all of us lifted up off the floor and the glory of the Lord covered everyone. Soon after, we were let down and got into intercessory prayers. The power that preceded that event was evident. Sicknesses and diseases were healed. As we went out, God gave us souls who decided for Jesus Christ. Amazing! That is what the Holy Spirit can do. As you yield to Him, as you allow yourself to be incubated by the Spirit, you will see the wonders of God. You will experience a recharge and a lifting.

The Holy Spirit helps to sharpen your sensitivity in the Lord. Wisdom and knowledge come from God. Increased wisdom and knowledge are made possible by the Spirit. For example, the natural man does not understand the scripture unless it has been explained to him. He reads the Bible with literal interpretation and comes to a conclusion that it is a Jewish literature. The man lacks an understanding, though a professor of religion. When the Spirit of God gets him on, incubates him, and breathes a life into such a man, he gains insight and his senses are sharpened. He begins to understand spiritual things in line with God's word. Across the professional divide and trades in life, God visits His people with some insights at baptism of the Holy Ghost. Senses are at full operating capability at the ascent of the Holy Spirit. On that last day of the feast Jesus said, **"Let him who thirst come, and I will give him of the waters of the Spirit."** Will you be willing to submit to the power of the Spirit and be incubated under His leadership and warmth? It takes a pregnant woman to understand the leaping of the baby. Until you have tasted, and become pregnant, you may not know the power of the Spirit.

Are you pregnant with a child? Has the Lord imputed some life in your womb? You ought to be pregnant with something, something bigger than your pursuit or your dreams or your ambitions. You ought to have the Holy Ghost inside of you.

5. The power of the Holy Ghost in a mortal man

He breathed into man's nostril and he became a living soul. The Lord wants to immerse us into the Spirit, to be baptized and 'consumed.' There is a power transcending the physical realm, beyond what political power can absorb and challenge. It is a power of the supernatural, a power that speaks to the spiritual world and tames it. This power is available to all who would yield to the invitation of God to be impregnated of the Spirit. Like Mary, you begin to carry the Spirit, the Son around.

Man: the habitation of God (God makes a home in man)

As this impregnation takes place, God begins to make home in your soul. Recall that when God created man, He breathed on him and he (man) became a living soul. The fullness of Godhead dwelt in man; man began to operate at full capacity and had control over other creatures. That control is dominion, power, and authority. This happened because God was living in man. The expression of the God-nature went forth and the aura and glory of the Most High was radiating through man. Notice that when Mary went to see Elizabeth, John the Baptist was already in the womb of Elizabeth. As Mary entered the house, John, still in the womb, leaped in worship, recognizing the presence of God.

In the same way Adam was endowed with power, was a carrier of the Spirit of God and, subsequently, all creatures obeyed him. When God implants His Spirit in you, other creatures will recognize Him. When Jesus approached the city of Gadarenes there was a man with an unclean spirit who dwelt in the graveyards and was such a violent fellow that no man was able to tame him:

"And they came over unto the other side of the sea, into the country of the Gadarenes. And when he was come out of the ship, immediately there met him out of the tombs a man with an unclean spirit, Who had his dwelling among the tombs; and no man could bind him, no, not with chains: Because that he had been often bound with fetters and chains, and the chains had been plucked asunder by him, and the fetters broken in pieces: neither could any man tame him. And always, night and day, he was in the mountains, and in the tombs, crying, and cutting himself with stones. But when he saw Jesus afar off, he ran and worshipped him, And cried with a loud voice, and said, What have I to do with thee, Jesus, thou Son of the most high God? I adjure thee by God, that thou torment me not." (Mark 5:1-7)

When the Spirit lives inside of you, everything and everyone ought to take notice, even the spiritual world and its demons. If this is not the case with your life, then something needs to happen to you. You need to be immersed and impregnated with the Holy Spirit. This is a sure way to live a victorious Christian life; to live in the Spirit. You find God living His life in you and through you. As the Holy Ghost, the Seed of God is planted in your heart, you are empowered to overcome sin and the luring appeals of the flesh. Sensual living and selfish cravings are greatly minimized; your focus is in heaven though you live on earth. Earthly appeals fade at the thought of the Spiritual home you are expecting and the urge to go after the program of God is pursued with every strength you have. Life begins to make sense and have a meaning. At this point, your thoughts are in line with the perfect desires of God. You think the way He thinks. His business is your business and your passion is all about heaven, souls, and the institution of heaven on earth. These happen because the Seed of God is planted in you. You are pregnant of the Spirit.

I was imagining this big God making a home inside of me. That is unimaginable. God dwelling in man and living there is the most unimaginable miracle; more so, to live in a once forsaken, filthy man. Ever since the regeneration and the habitation of the Spirit of God, I became a living soul. God promises to dwell (not visit) in me forever. This is unimaginable. Would you not want this experience; to live like God, to be a carrier of His Spirit? I invite you to the experience of being pregnant with the Spirit; the Mary experience. The Holy Ghost still impregnates people today. He is waiting for you. Get yourself ready for a baptism, for an infilling, and you will be grateful for the experience. That is the way to live. Get on your knees and ask Him to overwhelm you now!

CHAPTER TWO

MARY

The story of Mary to whom the angel said, **"Hail, thou that art highly favored, the Lord is with thee: blessed art thou among women"** (Luke 1:28), would be poorly presented if detailed attention is not given to the fact that this woman was just like any one of us and that her reverence and recognition were powered by God on the platform of grace and privilege, in contrast to the amplification of many religious garbs around this simple, but chosen vessel. First, the new testament of the Bible provides other Marys who in their different styles and occupations teach on other topics. Our consideration here is on Mary, the mother of Jesus Christ. However, other Marys in Scripture include:

1. Mary Magdalene (Matthew 27:56; Mark 15:40, 41)

- Received salvation (Luke 8:2)
- Showed gratitude (Mark 15:40)
- Showed up at the Cross (John 19:25)
- Was the first Christ appeared to (Mark 16:9)
- Received revelation (John 20:11-18)

2. Mary of Bethany (Mark 14:8, 9; Luke 10:39; John 11:1, 32); immortalized by Christ.
3. Mary, mother of James (Matthew 27:56; Mark 15:40; 15:47; Luke 24:10)
4. Mary, mother of Mark (Acts 12:12; Colossians 4:10)
5. Mary, disciple in Church at Rome (Romans 16:6)

Among the women of scripture, Mary was an extraordinary fellow; one who stood out above all others as the most blessed, most highly favored by God, and most universally admired. No woman in scripture is more truly remarkable than Mary, Joseph's spouse.

Mary's credentials:

Mary was sovereignly chosen by God—to be the singular instrument through which He would, at last, bring the Messiah into the world.

All generations would call her blessed by God (Luke 1:4). This was not made possible because she believed herself to be a saint or some sort of 'angel with a human face,' or a superhuman, but because she was bestowed with a remarkable grace and privilege. Mary's world recognized her and accorded respect to Jesus. **"Blessed is the womb that bore You and the breasts at which You nursed"** the crowd said to Jesus.

Mary, just another girl

True, Mary was blessed; she was an extraordinary woman among women but she was just a woman. She was born and raised like any other girl in Galilee, learnt her trade and had a desire to be married and bear children, just like any other woman. Her "blessedness" appeals to some religious caucus and misinterpretations alluding to her as a demigod or saint that transcends the human race remain a debate among the clergy. Mary was a mere woman who found grace and favor with God. Like a vessel, God chose her to fulfill His redemptive work for man. As a human, God worked through her to relate to man and bring the grand design of Sovereign and Eternal plan that was laid from the beginning. Some things are worthy of note here:

1. Mary herself is not the fountain of grace; Jesus is (Psalm 72:17).

2. Mary is not the long-awaited Seed of Abraham of whom the covenant promise spoke (Genesis 22:18). Jesus Christ is.
3. She does not translate our prayers to God as a mediator between man and Jesus Christ, then to God. Mary prayed to the Lord and even sought for her salvation. Many think of her as more approachable and more sympathetic than Christ. This is an error.
4. Mary was touched by the original sin of Adam even in her virginity. In Adam she inherited sin and lived with it. In error, she is revered as the perfect Madonna, supposedly untouched by original sin (because of her virginity, or maybe she was supposed to be a perpetual virgin).
5. Mary was not the Redeemer and never was made a Co-Redeemer with Christ. She was a channel, a vessel, so to speak, towards redemption.
6. She was not taken bodily to heaven, where she was crowned "Queen of Heaven."
7. Her role in the scheme of things was neither mediatory nor intercessory. When prayers are directed to her instead of to God alone, it becomes an error.

Mary was none of the above but we see a vessel who was yielded to the Lord for use. We see a human who God could reach out to and feel comfortable to pour Himself into and bless humanity. In Mary, we see an extension of GRACE and FAVOR for which until today, man has sought and prayed for. A close look at this young girl tells a story of one who was unassuming, yet simple towards her God. In the crowded schedules of life, there was serenity and purpose: to fulfill God's plan and be counted worthy of Deliverance with its promised Kingdom. Mary was one of those girls waiting for the fulfillment of prophecy. That lends to our situations today. This unassuming simple girl, a house wife-to-be, attracted God's attention. God visited her with a proclamation: "Hail Mary, full of grace..."

In our world of different mix of religions, we would expect a thunderous enchantment of the clergy or a heavy echo to the announcement or a political, class structured selection of who the mother of the Savior would be. God thinks differently. Assuming God requested of the High Priest the resume of all single girls in Galilee, against who the Lord should pick, I believe Mary's name would not qualify to be enlisted. She was just a girl. The same goes with you. Great grace was unleashed to us, a people without a God, headed towards destruction and without a purpose in life. Grace found us plateaued with our offended Maker and poured Himself inside of us. We could have been sniffed off with the wild wind; the devil would have made us a by-word; never to be remembered on the pages of history, but God preserved and saved us. Recall your foundation, your beginning, your exposure to witchcrafts, to demonic practices and wild partying. God monitoring your passage and endured great offense as you traded tackles with Satan. To you, He was a partial Judge. Indeed He is still a partial Deliverer. Such was Mary; the same with you.

God poured Himself into a jar of clay! He still does same today. When the Holy Ghost came on you, it was obvious that the container (YOU) was inadequate to contain Him. But God chose you to fulfill his divine purpose for humanity and to show His glory to the world; to encourage His Church and mature his people towards the second appearance of Jesus Christ. He chose you to do that; not necessarily for who you are or what you have done or the position He placed in your arm-beats, or the resources within your reach, or your ethnicity or tribal extraction; but because He just wanted to do that. God set His eyes on you, just like Mary. So we can come to terms with the fact that God chooses the waste and useless things of the world to show His glory and divine purpose; to make known His power and show case His plans for humanity. He chose Mary. He can choose you.

I remember Amos during the time of Israel's exile in Babylon. He was raised as a shepherd boy and grew up tending the sheep when God gave him a message for Israel. He was fast to do a disclaimer to his message and the validation or proof of concept to the claim that God called him, despising all the High

Priests and big prophets of his time. "I am not a prophet nor the son of a prophet but this is a message from the Lord...," was Amos' words to Israel. The same goes with John the Baptist. "I am not He that will come, I am a voice crying in the wilderness; prepare the way for the coming of the Lord; make yourselves ready for the coming of the Messiah; repent of your sins and make your crooked paths straight..."

2. A body thou hast prepared for me Hebrews 10:5-10 (Psalm 40:6-8)

God prepares men for His work. He is a God of order and makes clear the need to sanitize the vessel for His occupation. According to Psalms, the Lord was speaking to the ends of the Earth that He's got a vessel prepared for use to accomplish His work in man. He sought for a body to live in and then operate from. Like any venture heaven undertakes, there is always a vessel through which such projects are executed. Mary was chosen as the vessel prepared by God. This leaves us with the process of preparation. Was Mary taking some theological classes? Or was she under some mentoring and in-service program? Or was she just a house keeper? The fact that Mary was used leaves us with the perception that God can pick anybody, clean the person up and then, use. The details of work done are only known by God. There should be a preparation; then an offering of the body, then the use.

Be prepared (1 Peter 3:1-6)

Preparation for execution of any project is vital for successful completion. The adage that says; "if you fail to plan, then you plan to fail" tells it all. In the quest to be used by God to do His eternal purpose on Earth, there is the urge to jump the gun. God requires all men who aspire to work with Him to be prepared. A bishop must not be a novice because kingdom work is not for the wee ones. In 1 Samuel 3:7, the scripture states, **"Now Samuel did not yet know the Lord, neither was the word of the Lord revealed to him...and the Lord called Samuel again the third time..."** Why did the Lord call Samuel and reveal His mind to the young boy instead of Eli? Because the word of the Lord was precious (scarce; diminished); there was no open vision; the light (lamp) of God went out in the temple of the Lord where the ark of the Lord was" Samuel had not known the Lord. Because there was no alternative ear to speak to, the Lord chose Samuel, at least he was available. Except for emergent situations, the work of the Lord demands thorough equipping and preparing. As for Mary, I perceive she must prepared herself in all matters of godliness and righteousness. Mary's disposition would not have been to decorate herself with jewelries thereby appealing to the outer man at the detriment of her soul. The preparation for the body the Holy Spirit would dwell would definitely be clean. A body you have prepared for me! Which body? Who is the person to whom the Lord is asking to prepare Him a body? I think you are the one. A vessel of honor meet for the Master's use. This body is not the outward adornment with the most expensive jewelries of expensive cars or clothing or houses. This body is the purity of the inner man; the hidden man of the heart. As the Holy Spirit comes on a man, He begins to plough the heart and cultivates the Fruit of the Spirit in the man. This preparation is the work of the Spirit and so for many of us who desire to be enlisted in the work force of God, we must let the business of the world which has seized our attention and passion and begin to ask the Spirit to start a reengineering process of plowing and cultivating our hearts, preparing such for the work of His Kingdom. As God checks on a body to see if it is ready for occupation, He looks for a life with these characteristics:

- submit to one another
- holds chaste conversations
- having godly fear
- sick of adorning with the plaiting of hair
- wary of ornaments of gold

- true personality within the heart (pure and holy)
- preserving the incorruptible beauty
- an ornament of a meek and quiet spirit
- one that is precious in God's sight

To achieve the above, we must all work on the flesh; to flush out or kill the natural man (the old man). Mortify therefore your members... (Colossians 3:1), and bring to subjection the unruly desires of the flesh. As you obtain the Baptism of the Spirit and daily walk in obedience and newness of life, the life of Christ blossoms in your life and the Fruit of the Spirit manifests (Ephesians 5:22-25). The power to say NO to sin is received and your vessel is made ready for His use. Struggle against sin is no more because the power in the Word works effectually through your spirit and psyche to the soul and emotion. It grips you from the inside and there is a manifestation in the body. The power and glory released at Calvary comes to bear on the believer who accesses this resource. There is now no condemnation to those in Christ Jesus who walk not according to the flesh, but according to the Spirit of God. (Romans 8:1).

Such things as being:

- covetous

- proud
- gossip
- envy
- slanderer

are gone with the old man, Mr. Flesh. There is a new YOU and the glory of God is seen. You are ready to be offered for His use.

Mary offered her body to be used by the Holy Spirit

A virgin shall conceive a son of the Holy Ghost. In Genesis 6:1-8, we read of spiritual beings occupying human bodies; sons of God got married to daughters of men and consequently producing giants on Earth. The theological analysis of that scripture is not the intent of this book but we know that spiritual beings occupy human vessel. They fill a space and take dwelling in God's creation, including human bodies. As humans we have an option to yield our bodies to be filled by the Spirit of God or by some demons, the degree of occupation depends on the level of influence and indulgence you have with them. However the game goes, God does allow man to use his will to decide which game to play. Mary willingly accepted the visit by the Holy Ghost, offered her body to be infused by the Spirit and the Redeemer was born. We, on the other hand, are work men and tools in God's hand. He wants to use us but He must be given the permission to swing into action before any work can begin. Take for example, at our jobs, schools and offices; there are several niches that call for our expression and involvement. Human involvement in the kingdom business here on Earth go beyond the reach of Church walls or the call to "be a full time preacher" God desires that everyone finds a niche and a space in the vineyard to fully maximize our potentials and given talents to further push the frontiers of the gospel to reach out to 'unchurched' people around the globe. The need to spread out to unknown and uncertain terrains as offering of the body is a daunting task that does not sit well with empire-pastors and other clergy of our day. We are comfortable with fast-easy gains of preaching; not the making of a disciple. The Lord wants to make for Himself, a body. He searches through your ranks, just to find who to behold; who can be trusted and is available to handle the precious seed (the word of life). Will God find a body to use in you? The night is far much spent; the light shines in the morning. Come, prepare Him a body to use.

3. Believe, have faith in god against all odds (Luke 1:45)

When Elizabeth saw Mary at the door the two babies in the womb (one, six months older than the other) connected from the inside. John the Baptist bowed in worship and through Elizabeth came the word of Faith. **"Blessed is he that believes, for there shall be a performance of the things spoken by the Lord to the person."** In our walk with the Lord, there comes a time of extra contradiction around what we believe or what the Lord indicates to us by way of revelations. The Lord had spoken to Mary. He spoke to and gave Zachariah a sign concerning John. To the natural man these conditions were wary and hard to believe. First, Elizabeth had passed the age of child bearing; she was passed her reproductive stage in life but the Lord spoke and put the baby John in the womb. I imagine how Elizabeth felt with a supporting walking stick on one hand and a well rounded big belly with a baby inside, as she walked the isles. Society and her immediate communities must have wondered at the sight and circumstances and stories hitting the headlines on this pregnancy. In the midst of all these, her husband was truck, right inside the temple where deliverance is expected to occur, dumb. Tale bearers went to town to discuss Elizabeth; "the duo must have committed some terrible sins in the temple, no wonder, after all, they just bought a brand new SUV and a new house; that's money they stole from the Church treasury" "Why is Pastor Zachariah not speaking and why this sudden pregnancy at her age" "Something must be fishing" There must have been a tall tale in the city. All these Elizabeth and dumb Zachariah lived with; praying for the salvation of God.

As the day closed into the dews of the evening, Mary hurriedly came knocking at the door, excited at what was revealed to her by the angel; not knowing she was already carrying a Seed that would transform souls of men for many generations. The story that followed, though a prologue of the age-long hope for Israel's deliverance and salvation; would, to the tale bearers, be another addition and 'a substantial evidence to their argument against the prophetic word spoken concerning John and Jesus Christ. The two families had no evidence to tender, no witness to lay hold on to support or argue in defense to what said to them. The heard God speak; they believed the Word from the Lord. It takes a daunting, resolute faith, to stick to what you know was revealed. Many times, the revealed word and the spoken word make little or no sense to the natural man. The spiritual man lives in pain, trying to make the mind of God plain and appreciated. He agonizes to explain the word, the looming danger that will follow acts of wickedness of men. He speaks of love and compassion from God, providing for second chance to fix what has long been branded a norm and a culture in our society; but man would not listen. At the time Mary, the situation called for stoning; it was a hopeless case of disowning her; right from the nucleus family to the Joseph's family whose family tree and pride would not tolerate any act of blackmail. In all these, they remembered the visit of the Angel, the voice of God. Elizabeth reiterated:

"Blessed is he that believes, for there shall be a performance of the things spoken by the Lord to the person." "But without faith, it is impossible to please Him because whoever that comes to Him must believe that He is and is the rewarder of those who diligently seek Him out."

Faith is very important in the journey with God. Mark 11:22&23, speaks to that. Have faith in God, Jesus later told His followers. Faith in God comes to test, not when all things are going on as designed and planned. Faith is energized when our operations and schemes hit some rocks; when we seem to be drowning and life is at crossroads. The simple trust and reliance on the Father grows and develops deep roots when the going begins to get tough. Mary was in this situation; Elizabeth's situation was obvious. Who would their reports? Who would accept that without intercourse, a woman is carrying a baby? A baby by whom? And Mary would say, 'by the Holy Ghost" Unless the arm of the Lord is revealed to a person, spiritual things are hidden and sealed off of the eyes of men. There are moments of agony and despair. There are moments when you cannot explain to your group what the Lord is saying. Until there is an open vision, men will continue to grope in darkness. Only by faith can you move ahead, not bothered by the testimony of men. Since you believe the word of the Lord, there shall be a performance of that; a reality and manifestation to what you were told; to what you saw and what you have been instructed to carry on with in ministry. Truly, there shall be a performance, an actualization of those things the Lord spoke through you or some other person. Have faith in God!

Mary and Elizabeth believed against all odds. I discover that true faith comes to test when great things happen or about to happen. As the Lord set out with a program to save humanity, when the heavens rejoiced at the ground breaking program of a stately decorated YOU (at conversion); when a prophetic word went out on your coronation; hell set itself against that program and vowed to eliminate the lifeline God laid at the foundation. In all these, you ought to stand strong and unmoved. You stay the course and be determined to go through the faith test. You will come out of it a victor. God declares, **"Is anything too hard for me?"** You know the answer! When faith wavers and sometimes doubt comes in; be assured that God is in here to cheer your heart so you can sail to the other side of life. Assuming you have been beaten up and bruised; God encourages you not to cast away your confidence; your composure.

"Cast not away therefore your confidence which has great recompense of rewards. For ye have

need of patience, that, after ye have done the will of God, ye might receive the promise. For yet a little while and he that shall come will come and will not tarry. Now the just shall live by faith; but if any man draw back my soul shall have no pleasure in him. But we are not of them who draw back unto perdition, but of them that believe to the saving of the soul" (Hebrew 10:35-39 KJV)

Faith in pain and pressure (Hebrew 11: 12-40)

Ever experienced pain inside your spirit when all the people fail to understand your view point? For Mary, it was a show down of assault and an abomination for a girl to get pregnant without a spouse. She would have chosen to commit suicide, or to run away from home or to do some wired things regarding her state at that moment. Mary was one of a kind. In her lineage, maybe, there was none that has gone through this path of societal disdain or a scum at the heels of peers. She endured the pain and the rejection. Since pregnancy was and is owned by the man, Mary had no one to own her pregnancy, Joseph was thinking of writing a note to dissolve the engagement. As I write, it comes heavily weighted on me that a lady's heart is tender and soft; so soft that anything can go through it. Women are not created for the hard stuff, no, not when it touches the heart and emotions. At the birth and death of Jesus Mary must have suffered the greatest pains of her life.

Those were heart breaking moments of rejection and anguish and pain. You may be in the same situation. Bruised, beaten up and rejected by society and friends.

There is something about spiritual revelation: when God appears to a man, He is usually alone by himself. God shows up during moments of meditation or in a trance or vision. He speaks to His man at the separate moment, when all human wisdom and tactics have failed and there seems to be hopelessness. Most of the time, God is withdrawn in the midst of an excited, noisy, self acclaimed achievers. The moment God speaks, He speaks to individuals, to a listening ear. He speaks to one person at a time. The vision so received is a tool or proof that God is with you. Now how do you prove that God spoke to you to a materialist, self seeking people? Beyond reason, you have nothing to show as evidence. The world wants to see a sign; the people are looking for wonders and miracles. But the beloved of God still knows that God spoke to him or her. The only evidence you have is the proof in your heart and the voice you heard and like a dumb man filled with words, you cannot express the message to the understanding of the natural man. You are stuck in a sink, as it were. Mary was having this experience with her people and close friends.

As a preacher, it may be difficult passing out an information God wants to share with His people.

Some of the information may be a hard sell to the people but still they ought to be presented in a clear, succinct manner. There is congestion and rancor in the heart. Mary had a good share of that piece of rancor. At such a time, the scripture declares that Mary kept these things in her heart. Silence may be all you need to get to the next directive on what to do. Do yourself a favor, stop talking, stop complaining but get back to the author life who knows about all confusions and hatred. He will provide help out of the rubble. Learn to silent before your accusers; speak less of yourself and do not attempt to defend God. Let Him fight the scorn and rejection. Get back to your alter from where you got the message, and talk to Him. Something will eventually explode. Get back to work and keep the spirit alive! There is a reason why your electronic gadget has a mute button. Use your mute button. Wait, I say, Wait for Him to fight the fight of faith for you (Psalm 37:1-5).

CHAPTER THREE

JOSEPH

Joseph is probably the most neglected personality among those that touched the birth of Jesus Christ. As we search through Joseph's file, one thing we must remember is that between the time of Abraham and the birth of Jesus, forty-two generations were recorded in scripture. Typified by the following: Matthew 1:11-16

Abraham_____14_____David_____14_____
__Captivity_____14_____Jesus   3x14   =   42 Generations

It is not the intention of this book to get into some theological argument on the time that constitutes a generation or the differential in timing but to lay the fact that forty-two generations passed by between the call of Abraham and the birth of Jesus Christ, according to the Scriptures. That must be a long time.

The generations who came from Adam were ear marked to bring forth the Savior and Messiah who would later fix the truncated man. From Genesis 3:15 where God promised the restoration of man, Joseph was in the loins of his ancestors, was getting ready to be used to raise the Messiah; and provide guidance and instruction to the One who formed him.

First, Who Is This Joseph?

Josiah begat Jeconiah and his brethren ... during captivity (Jeremiah 22:24-30):
Jehoiachin
Coniah
Jeconiah
King Jeconiah with a Curse?
Many theologians have proposed reasons why King Jeconiah was cursed. I intend to deal with issues around a cursed man and if by any reason you feel you are under a weight of a curse, like Jeconiah, we would post a solution and offer a way out of such a curse.

Cursed?

Joseph's ancestors were kings. Jeconiah and many more occupied the position that does not decipher Joseph who was only a carpenter. At the lower level of the family tree, we see Joseph eking out a living with wood work. I have listened to many preachers deride Joseph as a man of low fiber, who came off the annals of poverty and was hardly recognized, albeit from an uncelebrated peasant carpenter. They believe that this unfortunate disposition of Joseph crawled from the curse levied on his fore fathers; at least, the curse filtered into the family and resonated on Joseph. Before we draw conclusions, may I take you to the beginning where God cursed the Earth. In Genesis 3:17, the Earth was cursed as a result of the sin of man. In Genesis 8:20-22, this curse was reversed. Out of the Earth, God declares that seed time, sowing time and harvest time shall not cease. If there is a curse hanging over certain lives, there is hope for deliverance and repositioning in the Lord.

However, it is important to mention that many a Christian suffer annihilation and decimation as a result of curses levied on them because of different reasons. Some of these are:

Vulnerable persons can be cursed: People with limited knowledge of the word of God or lack of knowledge of who they are in Christ Jesus can be subject to curses by a superior power. In Galatians 4,

Paul was rebuking the Church of God for backsliding back into the practice of religion (observing moon days, following the traditions of the Pharisees, insisting on physical circumcision before new converts were received into the body of Christ etc) as base and elemental to the faith. They were tossed around on doctrine, subjected to the whims of their 'sweet persuaders' and thus victims of their devilish traps. Such people are easily cursed by their intimidators when they fail to practice or participate in the doctrines of their masters. James calls this group of Christians 'babies' who are easily persuaded and tossed to and fro by every wind of doctrine. They look at themselves in the mirror and forget their facial fitting when they turn away from the mirror. These are vulnerable and unstable.

Self inflicted curse: When a man dishonors his parents, he disobeys the word of God. When he walks into demons and participates in their worship, he inflicts a curse on himself. How? In Ephesians 6:1,2 the Scripture says **"Children, obey your parents in the Lord; honor your father and mother so that your days may be long on Earth."** Obedience remains the key to spiritual excellence and maturity. We must obey our spiritual leaders, and work diligently to honor our biological or adoptive parents. Noah was drunk. He was naked and very much exposed. One child was foolish and watched the old man in his nakedness, had fun doing that; the other was wise. He stepped backwards towards the naked old man, took a linen and covered his father. To the wise, Noah pronounced a blessing and to the other, a curse. Suffice to say that we grieve the heart of our parents by what we think is right; we presuppose that they belong to the mundane world, a world whose era and ideas are antiques and thus have no use for the next generations (X-Gen). By this we insult them, abuse and neglect who and what they stand for. We refuse to care for our parents. Under this burden, the parent is in agony, in deep regret, in tears. Those tears translate to a curse on someone guilty of those tears and regrets and burdens.

When a person walks into a demonic environment without a covering of the power of God, the person will attract curses. If he chooses to engage in vile behavior against the word of God, then demons have an access into him. The person is subjected to a curse.

Ancestors induced curses: This happens when parents engage in demon worship or were given to slavery and slave trade; engaged in consulting spiritual powers for whatever reason; the worship of objects or universal or spirit entities. They belong to cults and initiate their children in the cultic practices. It is a case of parents eating grapes while the children's teeth are forced to stand on edge. No more! I have good news for you. Christ redeemed us from the curse. As much as you have submitted to

Christ Jesus, and daily walk with Him, you've got your back covered (Romans 3; 8:1-4; Galatians 3:10; Ephesians 4:8; Hebrews 5:7-10).

The man, Joseph

Joseph was not one of the men measured by material and number. His ancestral line of kingship notwithstanding, he was an uncelebrated young carpenter in Nazareth. His desire to lead a simple, unnoticed life with Mary comes on the heels of the fact that the wherewithal to cut into society's wealth lacked. He hoped for deliverance from Caesar's torment on Israel. Like most men of the East, Joseph had his age grouping friends. They talked about girls, about economy and future prospects. Joseph was definitely not removed from his environment. Unlike Samuel Elkaner, he lived as one of the boys in the community whose income and roots were known. He was one of the community Steelers. Soon he began to date Mary. The duo must have met in the temple or some place. But it is obvious that there was a fusion of both minds; a love that was beyond youthful hype and euphoria. There was communication and understanding. I think Joseph disclosed everything about his family, and Mary was full of energy and waited for the union; she waited for a home. The unfolding events about their marriage shows that trust was built at the beginning and their traditional marriage counsels preceded the temple blessing. As these events took place, Joseph was not given to 'discovering if Mary was fertile.' Thus, he kept himself pure and distant. He read from the scroll about his great grand ancestors who were cursed. He knew his family had come a long way through their rank and file and it was foolishness to try a stupid behavior that may lead to another curse. Joseph kept himself pure. He knew Mary was a virgin, a virgin he was going to be proud of all the days of his life; a spotless virgin!

Inside this exciting moment, Mary came knocking at the door. "Yes, my beloved, come right in," he answered. Behind the stall brick walled house laid three midsize chairs made of the woods of Lebanon; at the center of the living foray you find this oak rounded table that provided a central navigation for family communion at evening 'koinonia'. This time, it was in wait for when Mary would join him as a spouse. The wall was decked with the star of David, made of carved woods and other familiar paintings; a reminiscence of the very art and craft device from Joseph's apprentice days. The far end right introduces visitors to the lobby that extends to the courtyard garden where you find a mix of tools and equipment laying scattered, under citrus and mango trees. The West end leads to the kitchen. As a bachelor, Joseph was hard hit with miniature selections of kitchen wares. He is short of making meals and doing the dishes, an insider information as to why he needed Mary so badly and that soon to complement him in this department of life and family. Joseph's outlook, to say the least, describes a 'below average,' out of the rumble kind of guy who believes in his God for the next meal. In all, you could visibly make volumes of literature on this young man's willingness to fight on in life and obtain the remains of what hope has for him, at least through his chosen trade as a carpenter.

As Mary stepped in, and with the broadest cheer he could find, Joseph extended a warm welcome and Mary fearfully declared the impossible: "Joseph, I am carrying a baby." "Whose baby is that?" he must have inquired, furiously. There was silence. The play just began, a reality that would change the course of universe and, particularly, of Joseph as a father to the Creator of the Heavens and the Earth.

First, there was drama, then anger then a legion of questions fielded for Mary to answer in a single shot. But do not forget that the trust and respect they had for each other had not flown away through the window. What happened was not humanly possible; it was hard to believe a story of sort by mere "the Holy Ghost came upon me" testimonial. It was an insult to Joseph's high School biology class or an inert wisdom of the elders (who he thought through will call him for question over who owns the baby Mary carrying). As Joseph thought this, a mix of anger and resentment almost got him off guard. He held his peace; paced the living room. His head was full of consequences of "this act" and the social stigma that would bring to them. He thought of how his beloved would-be-wife was going to stand the shame of being stoned to death on the account of fornication or adultery by the Pharisees. Confusion, Anxiety; Perplexed man were the state Joseph found himself; sometimes thinking, other times regretting getting into Mary's life. It was obvious to Joseph that this could not be. He decided, after due consultations with some friends and elders, to ask Mary to go her way. It was obviously, a hard decision for the one you loved and had hoped will form a family with you. According to common wisdom, and as a gentleman in the community, he did not want a public specter on Mary. The putting away was decided. It was to be done secretly and without blemish or stain.

"Now the birth of Jesus Christ was on this wise: When as His mother Mary was espoused to Joseph, before they came together, she was found with Child of the Holy Ghost. Then Joseph her husband, being a just man, and not willing to make her a public example, was minded to put her away privily. But while he thought on these things, behold, the angel of the LORD appeared unto him in a dream, saying, Joseph, thou son of David, fear not to take unto thee

Mary thy wife: for that which is conceived in her is of the Holy Ghost" (Matthew 1:18-20 KJV)

"Then Joseph being raised from sleep did as the angel of the LORD had bidden him, and took unto him his wife: And knew her not till she had brought forth her firstborn Son: and he called His Name JESUS" (Matthew 1:24&25).

Traits we find in Joseph
1. Joe the carpenter?

Consider his genealogy as coming from a kingdom of kings, to being a carpenter. Think about an unqualified handyman with the Home Depot in your area who works on wood at call; how we regard them; how we sense cold shrills at their appearance to fix broken cabinet in the kitchen. In your mind, they earn less than they are worth and sometimes we think they are the architects of their misfortunes. We measure and evaluate men by material things and how much they wield in dollar terms; or by their class structure: who belongs to society's ruling class. Joseph was one of such. Although he was not on the street begging for food, you could see that the young man was not among the elites of a club. He was not classified; at least not even as a priest, nor a High Priest among whom the roll calls of Bishops of his days were nominated and ordained. Joseph was just one of those fellows in the community. Just in time,

God chose the weak thing, the outcast to raise His Child. Had God requested for a list of possible fathers to take care of baby Jesus, you know Joseph would not make the list. Lobbyist would go to work to enlist the ruling class. Joseph would have been too ordinary to be called; and such are some of you. Too ordinary; too far removed from the ivory towers of society; too low to be given an opportunity. At that lower level, God finds His choice for eternity's program. He enlists His general's to start with ordinary jobs under His watch; the way He started with Joseph.

"For ye see your calling, brethren, how that not many wise men after the flesh, not many mighty, not many noble, are called: But God hath chosen the foolish things of the world to confound the wise; and God hath chosen the weak things of the world to confound the things which are mighty; And base things of the world, and things which are despised, hath God chosen, yea, and things which are not, to bring to nought things that are: That no flesh should glory in his presence. But of him are ye in Christ Jesus, who of God is made unto us wisdom, and righteousness, and sanctification, and redemption: That, according as it is written, He that glorieth, let him glory in the Lord." (1 Corinthians 1:26-31KJV)

Has God placed His hand on your life to use for His glory? Has there been an instruction to execute a project and bring a change on humanity?

You may not qualify. You may not have the means to execute the project but God will show-case His glory through you and in you. God does not call the qualified, He qualifies the called. Like Joseph, pick up your tools and get to work, there you will see the Lord; an Angel will be assigned to you with a message!

2. No room in the inn

First Joseph was obedient to civil authority. True, Rome had annexed Israel, subjected them to heavy tax burden, yet Joseph was obedient with his relatives. They went to be counted according to their family tree. Before the road trip, people had booked for hotels and suites; made necessary arrangements to cater for friends and families. For Joseph, he had little to put down by way of upfront payment for any accommodation; no matter how small. Mary knew about it but still loved the man God appointed for her. Truly, the decision to travel on the donkey with other members of family and friends was, by itself, a stigma on the family because, news had gone round about the 'so called virgin conception' with Mary. Joseph knew all that. Mary was ready to swallow the bitter pill of scorn and disgrace. As they journeyed, gossips and fault finders must have jerked into their caravan and deliberately wanted to get them started on a conflict. Both kept their calm because they had heard from the Lord concerning their various situations. They had heard instructions from God on His program with them. They believed in the message, fully aware of its content and the outcome that would follow. They were carrying something that was bigger than message of the tax master. They saw beyond the tax instructions of Caesar; were not discouraged by what men said about them as they moved on. As the head count progressed, Mary was troubled and labor started. Her water broke.

It is noteworthy that this family may have slept in the open field or camp site and so when labor started, Joseph was confused on what to do. There was no room in any hotel or suites. Everything had been sold out. The clinics and maternity wards were all closed. Homes were fully occupied with families and friends. There was no space to do anything private, except the sheep stall. With the sheep and goats, Joseph and Mary had a good fellowship as she gave birth to BABY JESUS. What a testimony!

This brings to mind the fact that in any given appointment with God; with any engagement with Him, it does not matter the situation or location; as far as God is in it, the project or the mission will prosper. What is important is to have God's approval and support behind the work; then watch it grow. As you do the work of God in Ministry, it must be clear that certain things we see and know as advantages are not really the way we think. Take for example; location of a ministry. Environment or resource advantage does not excite God if He disapproves of that project. On the contrary, if you choose a not-too rich hive for a ministry, maybe a wilderness like John the Baptist's (Luke 3:1-3) and you have God's approval to occupy for Him there, you will make full proof of the ministry there. Right in the crib with goats and sheep, Jesus was born. Do not forget He was in the beginning with the Father and had the same glory as the Father; yet He came to the world through the manger. Has God called you to preach the gospel? You seek Him first. Stay with the Father and the Holy Ghost and the Son. This resource comes first before any other. In your chamber, you get the blue prints and make sure you have His approval. The search for men or money or material things for ministry is not the first resource in working for Him. Your location is not the marker for a successful launch; it is the assurance and knowledge that God is with you as you go.

3. He was a caring man (Luke 2:4, 5)

Joseph was a man in the making. Having been weaned from the teenage years through his study of wood works, he learned that a man starts to live when he begins to die to himself and all the ephemerals around him. He took responsibility as a man to see that Mary was first comfortable and secured. He took Mary along with him, being great with Child. I see faith. I see a man broken and remolded. I see a man who knows when God speaks. Or how can one explain the fact that a man whose fiancée claimed to have conceived of the Holy Ghost, accepted the 'insult' and 'shame' and went ahead to publicize the 'shame' and took responsibility to care for baby and mother?

Nevertheless he took Mary to wife, and assumed full parental responsibility for her child--was from the first in loco parentis to Jesus. Joseph here provides a good example of a husband man who loves and provides for his family even when there seem to be conflicts. He addresses the issue of men quitting when the going gets tough. Joseph was indeed a man who stayed the course and led his home, knowing that God will one day ask for accountability on how he managed the home affairs. He knew that whatever the demand of profession or ministry is, family comes first. It is the baseline of family that yields to the growth (structure) of all other additions in life.

4. Joseph was the high priest of the home

It takes the man to recognize that he is the High Priest of the home; to see beyond everyone else and thus to be able to sustain the program and vision at home. **"But while he thought on these things, behold, the angel of the LORD appeared unto him in a dream, saying, Joseph, thou son of David, fear not to take unto thee Mary thy wife: for that which is** conceived in her is of the Holy Ghost." (Matthew 1:18-20 KJV)

Men must see the way God sees. Most times, women see beyond men; they are gifted in discerning things and 'reading the hand writing on the wall' before anything happens. That is how females are wired. Such 'third eye' qualities of a woman are however not appreciated until there is a potency that adds to it. This is the vision of the man. As Joseph thought through the things Mary told him, the Lord appeared to him. I believe Joseph did not just take things at face value, he thought them through. The thinking process of a man may go deeper than the woman; he stretches to analyze things and weigh in options and consequences. He balances the act and often times, begins to find a solution to issues. That is the man; the way he is wired. But in all these, Joseph maintained the posture of the priest. He was open to God to speak to him. It was that visit by the Angel that settled all strife. It confirmed Mary's claim. As a man, I am quick at analyzing things, thinking deeper than I should but it is usually the Lord that helps by revealing and confirming things which my wife has hitherto alluded to. We should learn from Joseph. Suffice to say that Mary kept the things the Angel spoke to her in her heart. She would rather pray and discuss it at the best moment with Joseph. Assuming Joseph got upset (before the Angel visited him), I believe Mary would keep mute. She prayed down the

Lord to convince Joseph Himself; and He did. In the place of prayer, God translates the burden of a heavy heart to a simple, praise worthy moment; when the answer comes. Mary's answer to prayer and shame was heard. Yours could also be heard, and answered.

5. He saw the big Picture (Matthew 1:18-21)
Joseph saw something more than his circumstances. He had read the scrolls, the prophets and the psalms. He knew that beyond his present occupation as a carpenter, there was something bigger and more glorious on his way. He saw the big picture in caring and being the father of his Creator (a mystery that will take eternity to unfold). He knew that this big picture of things will change the way he lived, affect his chosen profession and alter the alignment of things he care for in his life. By faith, Joseph had a glimpse of things to come; especially when Mary relayed the message from the Angel: **"And His name shall be called Jesus for He shall save His people from their sins."**
That was enough information to close shop and wait for the manifestation of the Messiah from his home. Joseph was keen in realizing this dream; was full of expectations. It was this faith that propelled him to wait on God. As he waited, saw an angel and received instructions. You see how spiritual things build up. With a spark of faith, God draws closer to see if there is a deeper interest. When you receive the

word of life, God watches to see if it will be applied in your daily living. As you do so, He reveals more and even permits a vision (or an Angel is sent to visit). The big picture here is that Joseph was a part of the kingdom of God on Earth. He would not let go. This vision formed a part of him and thus affected almost everything that he did. Because God had laid His hand on him, it was obvious that that Hand sustained him. Joseph saw the big picture. This picture also helped him to manage the shame and overcome all offense from traditional Jewish culture that permitted putting Mary away.

If you see the big picture behind your spouse, her calling, her gifting, her offerings, her values...and the work God intends that you do on her (your assignment) as colleague in the work; then you will not put her away. You will see her as a gift and a work-in-progress; just as you are.

The driver in life is what we hold dear to. The picture we see determines where we go to and where our passion is. What we see and crave for will define our passion and where our zeal is directed to. The big picture before us tells any passersby where we headed; where we will end. Joseph saw something bigger than tradition or friends' opinion or family ties. He stuck with the vision God gave him; with the word of God.

What's the big picture in your life; What really drives your involvement in your church and family?

When pressure from peer groups and society mount on you, like Joseph, what sustains your vision? I personally have discovered that if any of the under listed items form your vision in marrying or engagement in ministry you would have formed a dangerous foundation. These include:

1. Sex
2. Money
3. Children/Kids
4. Career/Profession
5. Fame

    The moment any one of these is achieved or unable to be attained, you begin to find fault in your spouse or ministry; you want to remarry or start your own ministry. Alternatively where there is a lack or a short fall in any, you grudge and want a way out of it. Man's heart is deceitful and desperately wicked, who can know it?
    When we see the big picture of heaven, of our Lord Jesus Christ waiting for us at the marriage supper appointment then we subject all actions and activities under that search light. Joseph subjected his profession and other activities under the search light of the vision he saw. What do you see? Be careful that what you see and hear meet the demands of heaven and are able to appease God who will judge the living and the dead.

CHAPTER FOUR

THE WISE MEN

Points to Note
1. There is the place of Myrrh, Gold, and Frankincense
2. The Great Gift from above is Jesus Christ
3. The pains of giving and the joy of giving must be fully understood and practiced

Wise Men: this title designates an order, or caste, of priests and philosophers (called magi), which existed in the countries east of the Euphrates, from a very remote period. We first find the word in Scripture at Jeremiah 39:13, in the name "rab-mag" which signifies chief magi. This class is frequently referred to in the Book of Daniel, where its members are called magicians, and it is probable that Daniel himself was a rab-mag (Daniel 5:11). The order is believed to have arisen among the Chaldeans and to have come down through the Assyrian, Median and Persian kingdoms. The magi were, in many ways, the Levites of the East; they performed all public religious rites, claimed exclusive mediator-ship between God and man, were the authority on all doctrinal points, constituted the supreme council of the realm, and had charge of the education of the royal family. The practiced divination, interpreted auguries and dreams, and professed to foretell the destinies of men. They were particularly famous for their skill in astronomy, and had kept a record of the more important celestial phenomena, which dated back several centuries prior to the reign of Alexander the Great. They were probably originally honest seekers after truth, but degenerated into mere impostors, as the Bible record shows (Acts 9:9-11; 14:8).

    Nothing is said as to the number who came, nor as to the country whence they came. The number and quality of the gifts has become the foundation for a tradition that they were three kings from Arabia, and during the Middle Ages it was professed that their bodies were found and removed to the cathedral at Cologne. Their shrine is still shown there to travelers, and their names are given as Caspar, Melchior, and Balthazar; from the east (probably from Persia, the chief seat of the Median religion). Jews dwelling in Persian provinces among the Parthians, Medes, and Elamites (Acts 2:9) may have so prepared the minds of the magi as to set them looking for the star of Bethlehem. Beside the knowledge carried by captive Israelites the men of the East had other light. The great Chinese sage, Confucius (B.C. 551-479), foretold a coming Teacher in the West, and Zoroaster, the founder of the Persian religion, who is thought to have been a contemporary of Abraham, had predicted the coming of a great, supernaturally begotten Prophet; to these Balaam had added his prophecy in Numbers 24:17.

The wise men, the magi, were men from various educated classes. They were of noble birth, educated, wealthy, and influential. They were philosophers, the counselors of rulers, learned in all the wisdom of the ancient East. The wise men who came seeking the Christ child were not idolaters; they were upright men of integrity. They were men society looked up to for guidance and counsel.

According to legend in Western Christianity, there were three "wise men," their names were Melchior, Caspar and Balthasar, and they were of various ethnic or racial origin. However, Matthew's account of the magi's visit tells us none of these details. Since Matthew tells us that the magi brought Jesus gifts of gold, frankincense, and myrrh, popular imagination has pictured three gifts to be associated with three gift-bearers. In the East, tradition has generally pictured twelve magi. It was later tradition, not Matthew, who named the magi. A document dated to about 500 A.D. lists the names of Melchior, Caspar, and Balthasar, a tradition that has been maintained in Western Christianity. The 3 magi have been described not only as wise men, but also as kings or Persian priests and astrologers. The magi were given other names, as well, including Apellus, Amerus and Damasius, which were used in Peter Comestor's medieval Historia Scholastica (Metzger 5-15).

These wise men, however, had studied the Hebrew Scriptures and found a clear transcript of truth. I assume that Messianic prophecies of the Old Testament must have engulfed their attention, and among those, they found the words of Balaam: **"A Star shall come out of Jacob; a Scepter shall rise out of Israel"** (Numbers 24:17, NKJV). They were not naive to the prophecy of Micah: **"But you, Bethlehem Ephrathah, though you are little among the thousands of Judah, yet out of you shall come forth to Me the One to be Ruler in Israel"** (Micah 5:2, NKJV; (Matthew 2:5&6)). These wise men understood the time prophecy of Daniel regarding the appearance of the Messiah (Daniel 9:25&26) and came to the conclusion that His coming was near.

The magi were undoubtedly favored with a special revelation about the Baby and the star; given to them in a dream. The star, as one of the temporary incidentals of Christianity, faded away; but the Sun of righteousness which took its place in the spiritual firmament shines on, and shall shine on forever. The return of the star assured them that God would lead them safely and surely to the object of their desires. Their joy was a reminiscence of those who come from seasons of dark doubt or to say the least, from the dark corners of the Earth to the glories of light and faith would have had an unmeasured amount of grace bestowed on them. The star enabled them to find Jesus without asking questions, and bringing such public attention to him as would aid Herod in preventing his escape. Since the magi were guided by a star, they entered Bethlehem by night, and this I presume, contributed to the privacy of their coming and the safety of Jesus.

As they came into the house; the home of the carpenter, they received the shock of their lives (Joseph's wherewithal weighted at minimal) but for their faith in the revelation and the star, they must have thought they were mistaken, albeit; in the home of royalty; of the Son's empire decorated with spicy ornaments of gold but they saw the young child with Mary his mother as she was the only attendant in this King's retinue--the retinue of him who became poor that we, out of his poverty, might be made rich.

...they fell down and worshipped

Falling down to worship, with heads bowed is the usual Oriental method of showing either reverence or worship. It is safe to think that the manner in which they were led to Jesus caused them to worship him as divine. Their long journey and exuberant joy at its success indicate that they sought more than the great king of a foreign nation. The God who led them by a star, would hardly deny them full knowledge as to the object of their quest. They worshipped! How true of us today when we come into His presence, to surrender our intellect, our profession, our worth, our selves, and worship the One who holds our life like a porter holds and molds the clay.

    We should note their faith. They had known Christ but one day; he had performed no miracles; he had none other to do him homage; he was but a helpless Baby; yet they fell down and worshiped him. Their faith is told for a memorial of them. They worshiped him not as one who must win his honors; but as one already invested with them. When we come to Christ, let us come to worship, not to patronize, not to employ him for sectarian uses, not to use him as an axiom on which to base some vapid theological speculation but let us worship the One who put to rest the conflict between an angry God and a severely beaten down sinner; hopeless and confused. Let us worship the Messiah with all His glories come down; for who He is and majesties, His

immutabilities and His established governance among the nations and universe. Opening their treasures, they offered to him gifts. Oriental custom requires that an inferior shall approach his superior with a gift. For whatever reason, this is their culture and was played out with these wise men.
The wise men brought with them:

1. Gold: This is precious liquid metal that is mined from the weathered deposits of years of fossil sedimentations under the earth. It is the most precious metal and valued above all rubies. The gift of gold signified the kingship of Jesus and the relevance He brought back between God and man. Gold typifies the King and a highly exalted One, which position Jesus occupies and is honored with (1 Peter 1:18&19). The place of gold in the birth of Jesus tells a story about His power and authority in the overall scheme of things among humans. In the book "Digging for Gold" I laid out patterns and processes towards leading a fruitful life in Jesus Christ and thus, attaining or mining this Gold.

2. Frankincense: This is a white resin or gum obtained by slitting the bark of the Arbor thuris. The best is said to come from Persia. It is also a product of Arabia. It is very fragrant when burned. Frankincense represents the priestly office Jesus Christ occupies. (Exodus 30:34-38; Isaiah 43:23&24).

The fragrance from Frankincense is akin to the aroma that ascends the throne when priests burn the incense in the censer. It reminds me of the atonement and the sacrifice; the plea for mercy to the Father and the burdens priests have to bear for the people as they enter into the holy of holies, atoning for the sins of the people. Jesus seen as a priest (and we, the called out and sanctified ones) involves burden bearing (Exodus 28), interceding and laying our lives for the people as a kingdom of priests (1 Peter 2:9&10). It involves mediating between two parties: a holy God and sinful generation, pleading cases, the one and for the another. Frankincense typifies a priestly order that was exhibited by Moses when Israel sinned against the Lord and the Lord was angry, there was death in the camp. Moses immediately asked Aaron to run and gather the censer and offer incense to God so that the plague could stop. Aaron did and God was appeased. That is a priest. Jesus is our High Priest, scripture states that He ever lives to make intercession for us (Hebrews 7:24&25).

3. Myrrh: it is also obtained from a tree in the same manner as frankincense. The tree is similar to the acacia. It grows from eight to ten feet high, and is thorny. It is found in Egypt, Arabia, and Abyssinia. Myrrh means bitterness. The gum was chiefly used in embalming dead bodies, as it prevented putrefaction.

It was also used in ointments and for perfume; and as an anodyne it was sometimes added to wine. Myrrh exudes an aroma and reminds men about the death and burial of Jesus Christ. Myrrh represents the death which Jesus was going to experience for humanity (Mark 15:23; Luke 2: 34&35). Simeon, the man to whom God had revealed that the Messiah was on his way, was privileged to meet with this Child before he (Simeon) died. According to his prophecy, Simeon was in the temple at the time of Jesus' presentation and blessing. He tells the story of this gift from the wise men:

"And he came by the Spirit into the temple: and when the parents brought in the child Jesus, to do for him after the custom of the law, then took he him up in his arms, and blessed God, and said, 'Lord, now lettest thou thy servant depart in peace, according to thy word: for mine eyes have seen thy salvation, Which thou hast prepared before the face of all people; A light to lighten the Gentiles, and the glory of thy people Israel. And Joseph and his mother marveled at those things which were spoken of him. And Simeon blessed them, and said unto Mary his mother, Behold, this child is set for the fall and rising again of many in Israel; and for a sign which shall be spoken against; (Yea, a sword shall pierce through thy own soul also,) that the thoughts of many hearts may be revealed." (Luke 2:27-35)

What is intriguing here is that at a baby's dedication and blessing, a prophecy about how this baby's death was a high point in the blessing. It seems to me that the essence of this baby is his death; death by the cross and sword. **"Yea, a sword shall pierce through thy own soul also, that the thoughts of many hearts may be revealed."** Myrrh as a gift tells us that death was awaited and that through death, the power of Satan and sin in the lives of people would be destroyed. The purpose for which Jesus came is to destroy the power of sin, self and Satan. The tool set for the destruction was embedded in His death; albeit in the shed blood. This leaves us without contradiction that to live a meaningful life in Christ Jesus, there must be an experience of DEATH, without which, everything is ephemeral and transient. Death must occur in useful lives. Death to sin, death to self, and death to the world system. Until a man gets to that point of death (self, sin and world nailed to the cross of Jesus Christ) he may not have truly begun a new life in Christ Jesus. He is still the lord of his own life. So Myrrh is a good thing because it shows us the way Jesus was appointed and threaded. The same high calling looms before all Christians today. It is ours to take responsibility and obey as we follow after the model of Jesus Christ.

> What sacred fountain yonder springs
> Up from the throne of God,

And all new covenant blessings brings?
'Tis Jesus' precious blood.

What mighty sum paid all my debt
When I a bondman stood,
And has my soul at freedom set?
'This Jesus' precious blood.

What stream is that which sweeps away
My sins just like a flood,
Nor lets one guilty blemish stay?
'This Jesus' precious blood.

What voice is that which speaks for me
In heaven's high court for good,
And from the curse has made me free?
'This Jesus' precious blood.

What theme, my soul, shall best employ
Thy harp before thy God,
And made all heaven to ring with joy?
'This Jesus' precious blood.

When a prophetic word goes out, everything and everyone begin to exert all energies to accomplish (perpetuate) their attributes.

"Therefore the Lord Himself shall give you a sign; Behold, a virgin shall conceive, and bear a Son, and shall call His name Immanuel." (Isaiah 7:14)

The Lord created the heavens and the Earth by His spoken word. When He wants to accomplish a divine purpose among men, He speaks a word and programs begin to fit into that instruction. Since nothing exists in a vacuum, things respond to the call and mandate of heaven's order; they align themselves to the word of God, either positively or negatively. Nature and humans obey spiritual laws. They know when the Commander in Chief of heavenly forces and hosts speaks and so when the prophetic word went out, the Magi obeyed, the stars were stationed to lead the way. Concerning the baby Jesus, forces of darkness set themselves to kill the Messiah, God who decided to find habitation in human flesh. Our emphasis here is the action of the wise men, the stars and all their caravans. Why would wise men go out looking for a baby? History tells us that these wise men were not mean men; not men marginalized by circumstances and situations; they were men of high worth. Those familiar with the ways of God do not take Him for granted; He is not an age mate or colleague in the office. When God speaks, men ought to obey and go out with what was instructed to be done. Isaiah was quick to prophesy, Daniel asked to look into the glory that was to come and other prophets wanted a taste of this eternal 'menu' but were not allowed to participate. Yet men continued to search out the times and seasons. When the moment was ripe, the wise men from the East did not hold back. They obeyed and went, not knowing the way they went but were guided by the star.

The prophesy goes out to as many as would heed the call, like the wise men did heed: When God declares or gives an instruction, do you take it seriously? The pain heaven has always suffered is the neglect its messages have suffered; when men do pay attention to instructions and guideposts in life.
WHEN A PROPHETIC WORD GOES OUT, WHAT DO YOU DO WITH IT?
You Do Not Have a Second Chance to Make the First Impression!

As we hold this little discussion, there is an indication in your heart to go, do the work of the Lord to some folks who may be impoverished or homeless or maimed. The Holy Spirit speaks a word to your heart to represent Jesus Christ at your work place, to start a Bible Study or conduct School of Disciples program on a regular basis; to organize a Bible Club in your neighborhood or subdivision but you shun the voice and claim you have not been called; that you are not a preacher. The word of God has gone out to you through several channels and has urged you to go and do the work but it seems something else has caught your attention. The wise men were on top of their game because they were waiting; they searched for and were expectant for the revelation of a Messiah, a Deliverer. When the word goes forth, does it find a fertile soil; a home in your heart? The wise men knew better; they went out even through the night, though they were educated, rich and comfortable in their homes and empires.

> What sacred fountain yonder springs
> Up from the throne of God,
> And all new covenant blessings brings?
> 'Tis Jesus' precious blood.
>
> What mighty sum paid all my debt
> When I a bondman stood,
> And has my soul at freedom set?
> 'This Jesus' precious blood.
>
> What stream is that which sweeps away
> My sins just like a flood,
> Nor lets one guilty blemish stay?
> 'This Jesus' precious blood.
>
> What voice is that which speaks for me
> In heaven's high court for good,
> And from the curse has made me free?
> 'This Jesus' precious blood.
>
> What theme, my soul, shall best employ
> Thy harp before thy God,
> And made all heaven to ring with joy?
> 'This Jesus' precious blood.

When you receive a prophetic word, you should live with it and all it's about ... the consequences, the commitment and the blessings

Worship

Worship is central in God's demand from us. First we are created to worship and praise the Father for who He is, what He has done and even for what we are oblivious about. Worshipping the Lord in truth and in spirit leaves no room to the devil and lays to rest our fears and concerns. Music and worship go together. Worship, seen as an appreciation, not a duty, moves us into the inner chambers of the Father and gets us the buy-in to choicest things in life. Think about Jehoshaphat in 2 Chronicles 20 and Paul with Silas in Acts of the Apostles 16:24&25; there we see people who were not consumed by the immediate challenges and situations but saw a God who could be depended on for their situations. The wise men worshipped because by knowledge, they studied and researched of the coming Messiah and by experience, were there before Him. Nothing could have been more glorious. We ought to do the same because of the coming King and by our experiences of the new birth. In doing this we develop a hybrid of worship, praise and music for which Martin Luther gives his testimony like this:

"Music is a fair and lovely gift of God which has often wakened and moved me to the joy of preaching ... Music drives away the Devil and makes people gay ... Next after theology I give to music the highest place and the greatest honor. I would not change what little I know of music for something great. Experience proves that next to the Word of God only music deserves to be extolled as the mistress and governess of the feelings of the human heart. We know that to the devils music is distasteful and insufferable. My heart bubbles up and overflows in response to music, which has so often refreshed me and delivered me from dire plagues." (Here I Stand, 266)

Obedience

"**And being warned of God in a dream that they should not return to Herod, they departed into their own country another way.**" This suggests that as they came by night, so they were instructed to depart by night so that their coming and going might, in no way, betray the whereabouts of the infant King. They journeyed through the road, from Bethlehem to Jericho, and thus passed eastward without returning to Jerusalem. Because Herod had requested of these men to go and search out the Child and come back, with words of affirmation, but they did not yield to such evil plan. These men could have thought of a political position or some major contract from the monarch (Herod) that would fetch some good money. They were obedient to the word of the Lord; they journeyed eastwards.

Obedience remains the only key to unlocking access to God's presence. True test of faith lies in the willingness and ability to obey the word of God. The extent of use to which God will apply in a life is a function of the level of obedience He finds in a person, nothing else really matters before Him. The use of spiritual language or posture to becloud or rename an act that is contrary to Scriptural mandate does not suffice for obedience. In our society today, it is politically incorrect to refer to couples as husband and wife or the use of 'his' or 'her' has become mundane and past time. There seems to be gender equality and a neutrality of sexist construction. The word of God states, "in the beginning, God made them male and female" "a man must be husband of one wife (woman)" anything outside this order is coming from the devil and amounts to disobedience. Obedience to the word of God stands above everything else, including the claim to do things 'in the name of the spirit' for which, cannot run contrary to the written word. Political positions or correctness that trump on the word are evil and must be seen as handwritings of the emergence of the antichrist in our society. The wise men obeyed and were not mindful of their lives as they went the opposite way from Herod; undaunted, resolute, unbending for their faith and courage. Their testimony stands tall before us today; to dare the consequences and stand tall to defend the faith.

CHAPTER FIVE

HEROD ... Let My People Go!
Matthew 2:16-18; Jeremiah 31:15

- Why would Herod exert his energies in killing innocent, defenseless children?
- Why would a big Church go after a small fellowship to exterminate and wipe it out off a community or city just because the big Church wants to possess and occupy the land and thinks that the small Church is answerable (reports) to it?
- Why should a political caucus (kingmakers of a country) resist and vent their energies against any other person or group that wants to bring a change in the structure or composition of a democratic system?

The Herod behind me

August 1982, Wukari, Nigeria. I was in this restive town, south of the North East of Nigeria; today's Taraba State. The devil had stricken me with dysentery, diarrhea, and all kind of diseases. I had gone to pick my letter of admission from the Joint Admissions and Matriculation Board (JAMB), an agency responsible for examinations and admissions into Colleges and Universities in Nigeria. One one of those days I went to the Post Office to ask if the letter had arrived. Weak and dehydrated, I managed to walk to the Post Office but all along I was engaged in some serious prayers of deliverance and healing. Suffice to say that I was fasting, courtesy of the diarrhea. I asked God for healing and deliverance. Behold, right in front of the Post Office, this lady came to me, pleading that I should spare her life. I never knew her nor had any link with her at any time. She kept following and begging for her life. Meanwhile, I stopped and looked closely and saw that this lady was well dressed, with all the make-ups and well decorated scarf on her head. I imagined she was making a fool of a young man like me because she was beautiful and belonged to the upper class of society. Yet she kept pleading for mercy and her life. You could see fear all over her eyes. As she did, I kept my pace and told her I had no business with her, that I do not know her. At one point she paced backwards and was going away, afraid. I was at this point close to the door of the Post Office. She paced backwards. As I looked back after opening the door, she had disappeared. I could not locate her again. I went into the Post Office, asked for my letter and went home, still sick. I knelt down to thank the Lord for the day, and something happened to me on my knees. I became well and fit again. All the sicknesses had gone, in that split moment. The devil came to destroy, but God gave me victory. Praise the Lord!

I travelled to see my father in Uburu, Ohaozara Police Station, at least to present my letter of admission. He was elated and asked that I should make some African soup for him. I went to the evening food market to buy ingredients for the soup. On my way back home, I stepped on some object in a small hole. The story of life started to change immediately. It was obvious that my body started swelling up. There were bumps all over my body. I was doubling up in size. I knew the devil had struck again. I had stepped on some 'voodoo' African medicine, say a poison, placed by some fellow. Maybe not necessarily for me, but I was a victim. But the battle had just begun. I went straight into prayers. It was another prayer of deliverance. Three days of fasting and prayers. Interesting here was that I did not know any Christian brother to join me in these prayers. So as my siblings went to school, my dad went to work, I locked myself up in the house, praying. I knew help must come otherwise I was going to die. As I prayed, my body was getting back to normal and on the third day, I was completely healed. My dad could not believe that but agrees with me that there is power in prayers. The devil came to destroy, but God again gave me victory. That was Herod in my early life as a Christian. He knew there was a declaration by God concerning me, a purpose for my life, and he wanted to exterminate it.

This could have been you, but God would not let him. The many Herods on Earth will be destroyed in the name of Jesus. As we conclude with this last chapter, my prayer for you is that you will experience a turnaround in your life and begin to live a complete, new life in Christ Jesus. You will know that enemies of your soul have no right of occupancy and you, being a son or daughter, occupy a vital place in the heart of your Father.

5.1 Points to note!

As God sets out to accomplish a divine purpose, Satan begins to exert his energies to fault the purpose. For everything the Lord plans to accomplish in a life, especially the life He chooses to show case, there is usually a word, then a plan, and a plot by heaven to arrange for all the processes for that life to be where and what God wants it to be. For Jesus, the prophecy went out and soon that was declared, spirits convened a conference. It was a conference to exterminate the plan for redemption;

to put to death the Son of God and change God's plan for creation. Herod was already established in his kingdom and Rome was backing him up in all ways possible. He had all the support and resources needed to policy decisions. In the spirit world, forces could not just hold their peace because a Child of destiny was born. This Child will revert the course of Earth that got a hit since Genesis chapter three. Forces of darkness had gathered to end this project God was embarking on.

In our daily experiences in life we are engaged in many fights against evil spirits; spirits that yield to destroying the good intents of God on lives. They come to us through human agents or somewhat, through objects but however they show up, their underlying operator is the devil. These forces obtain instructions from Satan to undo the useful life; to ruin God's investment in our lives. Concerning Jesus Christ, it had been declared what His mission was and those evil forces were aware of this. To this end there was a stirring in Herod's heart to be used to stop the mission. Knowing this therefore, Satan will always put up an assault against the useful life since he knows there is a preparation and somehow, one day that useful life will be an agent of his demolition. This is why God makes us to know that we must be battle ready soon after we yield our lives to Christ. The Lord enjoins us to fight; a fight that lasts a life time; a fight of faith and victory over the works of darkness.

"Finally, my brethren, be strong in the Lord, and in the power of his might. Put on the whole armor of God, that ye may be able to stand against the wiles of the devil. For we wrestle not against flesh and blood, but against principalities, against powers, against the rulers of the darkness of this world, against spiritual wickedness in high places. Wherefore take unto you the whole armor of God, that ye may be able to withstand in the evil day, and having done all, to stand. Stand therefore, having your loins girt about with truth, and having on the breastplate of righteousness; And your feet shod with the preparation of the gospel of peace; Above all, taking the shield of faith, wherewith ye shall be able to quench all the fiery darts of the wicked. And take the helmet of salvation, and the sword of the Spirit, which is the word of God: Praying always with all prayer and supplication in the Spirit, and watching thereunto with all perseverance and supplication for all saints." (Ephesians 6:10-18)

To get through life, there is need to understand that it is akin to enlisting in war. A war that is a smooth sail if we hide under the Supreme General of Armed Forces of heaven. He is Jesus Christ who proved Himself faithful by the war He devastated the kingdom of darkness and made a public show of them all at Calvary. So the battle is fought and won by Jesus Christ. All we need to do is to stand in His place and obtain victory by faith; to retreat and hide behind His all-paid-for ticket to obtain victory.

"For though we walk in the flesh, we do not war after the flesh: (For the weapons of our warfare are not carnal, but mighty through God to the pulling down of strong holds;) Casting down imaginations, and every high thing that exalteth itself against the knowledge of God, and bringing into captivity every thought to the obedience of Christ; And having in a readiness to revenge all disobedience, when your obedience is fulfilled. Do ye look on things after the outward appearance? if any man trust to himself that he is Christ's, let him of himself think this again, that, as he is Christ's, even so are we Christ's." (2 Corinthians 10:3-7)

2. You must know the plans of Mr. Herod against your life

Secret things belong to God and only the ones revealed can be acted on by man. Obviously when the evil one plans his plot it is only the Lord that can depose him of such intents and expose the schemes to His children. When Herod planned to kill Jesus, God was aware of this plan. So God overturned his schemes and revealed that Joseph; the head of the home under whose care Jesus was to be raised.

"Now when they had gone, behold, an angel of the Lord appeared to Joseph in a dream and said, "Get up! Take the Child and His mother and flee to Egypt, and remain there until I tell you; for Herod is going to search for the Child to destroy Him." So Joseph got up and took the Child and His mother while it was still night, and left for Egypt. He remained there until the death of Herod. This was to fulfill what had been spoken by the Lord through the prophet:" "OUT OF EGYPT I CALLED MY SON." (Matthew 2:13-15 NIV)

Joseph was asked to take action immediately. He did. In our walk with the Lord, Herod comes in to kill, to destroy and to steal (John 10:10) but we must know that the plans of God for us to give us life at its fullest. When the devil plans a scheme or before he does, it is very important to seek the Lord on a regular basis so that we will have a blue print on the path He wants to take us through and also to reveal the hidden things spirits of the underworld are hashing out against the Lord and his elect. By this we would be better equipped to handle life's situations when they come.

The race we are engaged in is not for the swift, it is not for the strong neither is it for the smart and affluent, but it is by the grace and provisions of the Almighty God. Sometimes the Lord may even choose not to reveal what comes up next and simply allows circumstances to come our way by way of tests.

In all things you ought to remember that the seed in you, (the useful life) will not be eliminated at the budding stage; it must bear the fruit for which the Lord destined to bear. For Jesus, God was about a business in the world. That business was to atone for sins; to save humanity and restore man to his original place in God's scheme of creation, as far back as the decision to make man in the image of his creator was made. The default prototype was a combination of the DNAs of God the Father, God the Son, and God, the Holy Ghost. This comprised whatever the FATHER, THE SON and THE HOLY GHOST represent. That was the original model for man. Since this plan was set in motion, God was particularly involved. When you embark on projects God has His eyes on; that is to say, He is particularly involved in (I mean such projects that touch heaven and have eternity in view; ministries that eat deep into His heart; that count on the scale of eternity) God gets some attention and does the extraordinary. He goes gaga and defends His name against all odds. Suffice to say that God must be amused when we are involved in frivolities and things that have an impact on the world system and sensual cravings; that amplify ego and pride; even if they are done in the name of church or preaching.

For the useful life, God is particularly involved. He reveals His mind or exposes schemes of Satan so that their mobilizations are foolishness, yielding nothing to their dismay. Pray that the Lord reveals information to you. It is comforting to experience this with the Lord.

"If a trumpet is blown in a city will not the people tremble? If a calamity occurs in a city has not the LORD done it? Surely the Lord GOD does nothing Unless He reveals His secret counsel To His servants the prophets." (Amos 3:6&7 NIV)

Before you argue that this access to God's secret is exclusive for prophets, may I introduce a man who came from the heathen nation of Ur of Chaldeans; whose extraction had nothing to do with God or whatever He stood for and had all his life worshipped idols and sun gods. God reached out to him; to reveal Himself to him. He was Abraham. At a time in his journey with god, the Lord has this to say about Abraham:

"The LORD said, "Shall I hide from Abraham what I am about to do, since Abraham will surely become a great and mighty nation, and in him all the nations of the earth will be blessed? "For I have chosen him, so that he may command his children and his household after him to keep the way of the LORD by doing righteousness and justice, so that the LORD may bring upon Abraham what He has spoken about him." (Genesis 18:17-19 NIV)

Knowledge of the secrets of the enemy is an added advantage in our warfare. As the Lord wills, He reveals secrets. To know the secrets of your enemy and engage in combatant operation is a good tool to obtaining victory in battle. Go back to God, ask for the secret things of God and they will be revealed to you.

3. You can be delivered from the kingdom of darkness today! (Isaiah 49:22-26)

When Herod posted a deceit and asked the wise men to go search for Baby Jesus and bring back words to him so that he could go and worship likewise, it was a ruse and a ploy. According to Jeremiah 31:15 and Matthew 2:13-18, Herod slew all children under the age of two, because the wise men had fooled Him. The influence and scars Herod inflict on lives remain with us in this age, especially when we look at the truncated life styles of the people; their altered psyche, and emotions. Everything seems to be out of joint. When Mr. Herod identifies a useful life, especially the life destined to deliver good news to the people or has been marked out to influence generations with gifting, he is poised at destroying that life; more, when Rome (represented as the Headquarters for Herod) has given powers to enable the onslaught and gained substantial occupation. On the other hand there may be some who, out of zeal, walked into the lion's den. They literally allowed the devourers to invade their habitation as a result of what they got themselves in or what family ancestors did. For example, a man builds a business empire with money made out of slave trade, killing human beings or making several visits to shrines and blood houses; a family tree is aligned with witchcraft and demon worship (evoking the powers from the sea and ocean, making consultations with the dead and spirits in the grave yards; engaging in human trafficking and the practice of sorceries, cults and various forms of religions that do not take root in Christ Jesus). To these people, Satan has a claim on their lives because they broke the hedge, the serpent will surely bite them. These are the lawful captives of the devil. Here is good news for the lawful captives:

"Shall the prey be taken from the mighty, or the lawful captive delivered? But thus saith the Lord, Even the captives of the mighty shall be taken away, and the prey of the terrible shall be delivered: for I will contend with him that contendeth with thee, and I will save thy children. And I will feed them that oppress thee with their own flesh; and they shall be drunken with their own blood, as with sweet wine: and all flesh shall know that I the Lord am thy Saviour and thy Redeemer, the mighty One of Jacob." (Isaiah 49:24-26 KJV)

Jesus came to deliver you from the Herod of today. The Lord is saying that He will surely deliver you from oppression and hate. Though your past has been traumatic and painful; everything has gone south, it seems; and there is hopelessness with Herod at your back, almost taking hold of your life, there is hope for you. Before now you thought God has forsaken you and your ancestors' sins are haunting you. As much as you believe in the Lord Jesus Christ, you will be saved. Here is the promise you can count on:

"Then the word of the Lord came to me saying, 'What do you mean by this proverb concerning the land of Israel saying, 'The fathers eat the sour grapes, But the children's teeth are set on edge'? As I live,' declares the Lord God, 'you are surely not going to use this proverb in Israel anymore." (Ezekiel 18:1-3)

Jesus came to destroy the works of darkness and perpetuate His kingdom on Earth. You are an embodiment of the kingdom of God. Start a prayer, get into a closed space and talk to God as we continue.

5.2 Why Herod; why the hate?
1. Prophecies in play

Like Jesus, there was a prophetic utterance concerning His life, ministry and the value He was to deliver on humanity and the kingdom of God. It was ingrained and clear to all spirits and so they went to war. There was agitation and riot. Even after so many trials to eliminate Him, Hell was undaunted in their search to kill Jesus. Spirits were not appeased. Herod was a human being who yielded his body to be used by the spirits (just like believers in Christ Jesus yield their bodies as home for the Holy Spirit). Your case is not different. The day God delivered you from the curse and condemnation of hell spirits have in a conference determined the best strategy to kill the seed of God inside of you. There is a resolute will to undo you but thank God we are not condemned because, there is now no condemnation to those who are in Christ Jesus, who walk not according to the desires of the flesh but according to the Spirit of the living God.

Jesus gave a parable on the talents and their various recipients. The Master went on a long journey into a far country to receive for himself a kingdom and promised to return (Luke 19:12). He charged to occupy until he came back. He distributed talents and gave them ability and resources to take advantage and seize every opportunity to establish a rule and an order on Earth. "Occupy until I come back." We see in verse fourteen that the citizens were silent and muted until the Master left the scene and ascended. Then to these harmless folks He had given orders, the people came crying wolf.

"And he called ten of his slaves, and gave them ten minas and said to them, 'Do business with this until I come back.' But his citizens hated him and sent a delegation after him, saying, 'We do not want this man to reign over us." (Luke 19:13&14)

Why would they not have Jesus reign over them? Simple: His kingdom is different from their kingdom; His values are opposed to their values; His care about is opposed to their sensual cravings. There is a prophetic utterance on your life: "that a child is born to change the tide or course of order in your family or community and that child is carrying a seed of God (the word of God and the Holy Ghost)" This seed in you (call it an emblem or a flag or the seal of the Holy Spirit) sends cold frills to the enemy. This is the reason for the hate. Does that imply that you should melt before them? NO! The word says, "Occupy until I come."

2. Fear of dethronement

Herod was afraid of being deposed of his position as one in-charge of Judea. "Power corrupts and absolute power corrupts absolutely" they say. Herod's disposition did not make room for alternatives. Rome had annexed a number of countries and Caesar was in-charge. He had appointed relatives to head different cities and nations. The possibility of a job opening for Herod was remote if there should arise a new King over Israel; moreover, Israel being a cash cow to Rome (remember that Jews are known for hard work and the blessings of Abraham rests on the land, animals and labor) so there was this economic power Israel had. This cash cow (tributes to Caesar and Rome) would be something Herod dared to lose. Again his loyalty to Caesar and all the pride of "the man in-charge" definitely was something that must not be allowed to go. Herod feared being dethroned.

According to my grandfather's idiom; the bird in hand is worth more a million in the bush seems to make sense when one considers the fact that because the world and its people has no hope beyond their existence here on Earth, they hold tight to the things of this world. Some vent their energies on these things and would possibly die, fighting for a possession. Material things, power, money and ego (pride) seem to run the course of the world. Since these define men and place them on the pivot of human acceptance and acclaim, they are willing to die in combat, to possess or reclaim these vantages. So we begin to understand why the hate has gone bizarre; after all, we claim we are not of the world.

Fear of the unknown can cause a man to do the unimaginable thing; and truly the Scripture attests that fear has torment (1 John 4:18). May I ask you, in your job or position, is there any form of fear in your heart? Are you engulfed in any sense of insecurity about your ministry or position as a Bishop or Senior Pastor? If you are in this struggle, then you have a problem. You need help. Deal with this fear now! Seek for a mentor.

5.3 Pharaoh would not let the children of Israel go

1. He is a task master - An extortionist; a slave driver; enjoys power over the people:
The devil does not think good of anybody. In the book of Exodus, the Israelites were devastated and maltreated; were subjected to slavery and hate and when they cried to God for help in chapter two, God heard their cry. He sent Moses to deliver them from oppression and bondage. Pharaoh would not let Israel go to a land God had prepared for them until after long show of power and glory. Naturally Herod or Pharaoh would not want his captive to gain freedom. That would demean his ego and authority but when God sets a man loose from oppression and power of sin, nothing can enslave or hold the man back from fulfilling designed destiny. Herod, being a task master, enjoys the throne, courtesy of a preoccupation and thus the power Rome mates out to its annexed nations. Rome with its representative (Herod) felt that power can be flaunted and abused. So at will, a call is made 'to go bring the Baby' and soon after 'to execute all male children aged from three month and above. Task masters rule by marshal law. They issue commands that are contrary to divine order. They feel that power bestowed on them is used to intimidate others and fan the embers of their pride. In the Church, we find such tasks masters who levy struggling members to acquire for themselves properties and fame. Such members

being intimidated with some spiritual language and fear, yield them. They live all their lives in fear and eroded self worth (Hebrews 2:12-14).

2. Israel was the cash cow (chicken being raised for the day of slaughter):

The other reason why Herod or Pharaoh would hold tight to his victims is because the victim is a cash cow; an instrument preserved to make money or create wealth for the master. Like in the days of slave trade, slaves were branded for the good of their masters. They existed to work without due regard to human life, for the whole purpose of making money for their masters in the plantations or mines or wherever the master chooses. In the US today, the middle class exists to work and pay taxes so that the economy is sustained. They work for the very rich and the very poor to enjoy their labor, courtesy of the tax system. In other instances, institutions or movements engage in sending new convert Christians overseas in the name of Church planting with the aim that such young Christians indulge in some effort that gather people and insist on raising money (by whatever means) to be remitted to the headquarters who sent these new Christians abroad. Like Israel, these are the cash cows whose Herod would hold on to their lives, until all blood is drained off their system. Such life style is not sustainable. It is living in bondage. You need to be delivered if this is your story. If there is a Herod in your life who thinks or even casts a spell on you, indicating that you are forever tied to his gain and never investing in your life or Church or Community, then you must be delivered from that Herod. The enemy's agenda is to kill, to steal and to destroy. He comes to steal what he did not invest in your life, home, ministry or your community.

3. Herod would not transfer power; not interested in fostering a legacy but would want to kill the seed in you:

True leaders invest in their menthes and provide for the development of their students. Since they were God-ordained, their grip on power is loose because, first, they did not seize power or maneuver themselves into office. They knew they were called to serve. Opportunities to serve their communities came from God and they respect such mandates. Their calling was from God (Galatians 1:1&2) not orchestrated by man nor according to the will of man. It was purely from God. For the Pharaoh who represents an agent of Satan, his is a fierce, arrogant display of power. He goes to undo the people, to cheat and gather wealth and would not see power as transferable. Like Pharaoh, most African leaders, cling to power for more than thirty years because they see themselves as gods and 'created to rule' others. Their lives are tied to aprons of power;

having no alternatives and engrossed in the filth of corruption. Their heart melts when an opposition or a contender aspires to the throne. Jesus, the King of the Jews was born. His chemistry was not to constitute a kingdom on Earth, nor to depose Herod, but because the understanding of Jesus' kingship is not given to natural men, Herod concluded that his kingdom was to be taken. When men are afraid to lose their positions, ministries or personalities; then something is wrong. That fear alone is worth checking out because 'fear has torment' living within the heart. (1 John 4:18)

It is this fear of deposition that causes men to kill any seeming or real opposition. This opposition is the Spirit of God that runs against the current tide of the world system, the schemes of evil in the world. The seed of God you carry cannot contain the mess and decay around the world and so, when you show up, there seems to be commotion, an opposition; they simply begin to say: "we would not have this man reign over us." The grip on power and material things in life, (without any recourse to a hope and an enduring home in heaven) leave men without any option but that which they see and handle. The fear of losing "a bird in hand that is worth more than a million in the bush" drives men to killing fellow pilgrims in the war to gain it all. Had Herod seen a glory that was revealed, a Child born to deliver men from their sins (not from Rome and its annexation) he would have thought differently. Maybe, in your office or factory you just realized that a colleague is getting promoted or he is adding value to some job functions and management will soon promote him. You are bitter; then engage in gossip, plan to get rid of him and of course, you succeed. You are playing Herod. Herod's kingdom is of this world, his time of reign is determined, so he fights to gain it all while it lasts. God's kingdom is everlasting, it may suffer intimidation and hate momentarily, but not for too long. The Lord is the Governor among the nations.

4. There is a kingdom of Herod and the kingdom of God:

Since Herod's kingdom was of this world and all that mattered to the ruling party was to establish a reign that had its lifeline from the cosmos (materialism and political power), it becomes imperative that we look closely at the picture this kingdom paints and make enough provisioning to escape its grip and appeals. Jesus said that His kingdom was not of this world. Paul wrote to Timothy in this manner: **"Do not love the world or the things in the world. If anyone loves the world, the love of the Father is not in him. For all that is in the world—the lust of the flesh, the lust of the eyes, and the pride of life—is not of the Father but is of the world and the world is passing away, and the lust of

it; but he who does the will of God abides forever."
(2 John 2:15-17)

What then is the kingdom of this world and how do we know when we travel off the path to the kingdom of our God? The following table shows clearly, though not all inclusive, the differences between the two kingdoms in our daily choices and different departments in life.

The Two Kingdoms as Seen in Civil Society

1. What is there for me in this scheme?
2. I must make money by whatever and any means possible.
3. My political stand is defined by what gets me elected into office.
4. Life is about what you get out of people, program or projects; the denominator is the dollar.
5. There is no absolute in ethics or morals in business; the end justifies the means.
6. I must get what I want, when I want it and how I want it. I have no obligations to anyone.
7. Success is seen in what you have, who you are and where fame and acclaim have met you.
8. I am the boss; whatever I say stands in this office. You are an employee under my payroll.

9. I do not care about values and beliefs. Man is what he makes or does not make for himself. Everything depends on what you can handle.
10. God is an euphemism. Hell and heaven are here on earth.

The Two Kingdoms as Seen in the Church

1. I am redeemed to be rich, blessed to be happy. That is what I am created for.
2. Anointing without money translates to annoyance in ministry.
3. I must make it (money) in ministry by force or by fire; my God is not a poor God.
4. Our Church is known for mass production of men known for their wits and grits for material possession
5. Truth is really subjective, there is no absolute. Bible is only a guide, not the whole truth. Jesus is not the only way to God.
6. Whatever religion you belong, all God wants from you is to be a good person.
7. A good Church is known for its programs, music, shows, outdoor activities and community involvement.
8. I am called to make men rich (financially) and appeal to emotions and psyche so that people do not get hurt again.
9. We love people to the point that we cannot begin to insist on a certain way to live (choices) or dictate

who their spouses are; there is no such thing as man or woman, just address them as 'significant other' or 'spouses'.
10. The Holy Spirit is an influence, a staged drama and belongs to the Bible times, not now.

The Two Kingdoms as Seen in the Family (Home)

1. Everybody has equal rights and privileges in this home.
2. My thing belongs to me, there is no trespassing. I have my space, you have yours.
3. I am so proud of my job and profession. Nothing comes in between, not even my family.
4. My husband (wife) is such a terrible person. I will give him (her) a death certificate; wouldn't stop at a divorce document.
5. I am in this marriage for what I gain out of it, remember, I am the King's kid.
6. I took a vow: 'for better, for richer; in wealth and in happiness; forever happy and blessed" I stand by this.
7. I thought I was going to change her (him), she (he) is like every other lady (man) on the street.
8. I am not going to have babies (my pets can suffice) because I have only one life to live and must enjoy it to the maximum.
9. I do not have to disclose everything to my spouse, some secrets may be necessary against the rainy day.

10. Respect and love are reciprocal outcomes. She respects me, I will love her. He loves and provides for me, I will offer my body to him.

"And do not seek what you will eat and what you will drink, and do not keep worrying. For all these things the nations of the world eagerly seek; but your Father knows that you need these things; but seek His kingdom, and these things will be added to you; but seek His kingdom, and these things will be added to you. Do not be afraid, little flock, for your Father has chosen gladly to give you the kingdom. Sell your possessions and give to charity; make yourselves money belts which do not wear out, an unfailing treasure in heaven, where no thief comes near nor moth destroys. For where your treasure is, there your heart will be also." (Luke 12:29-34)

5.4 Satan came to steal, to kill and to destroy

One common denominator in the overall schemes of the evil one is that he comes to steal, to kill and to destroy. Whatever he does, no matter how religious and glamorous, whenever there is an opportunity, he subtly indulges in these nefarious activities to undo his victim.

Stealing is native to Satan because in our relationship with the Father, he was not a part of our salvation and redemption program. When the devil tricked Adam and Eve, it was obvious he had an eye on their descendant and thus was buying into a future return to destroy our destiny. The saying that goes, "all that glitter is not gold" is true of the devil. In a subtle and invasive style, the enemy of our souls creeps in with fancy words and luring suggestions to have us indulge in acts too dangerous for heaven to accommodate and too risky for grace to cover.

The result being that the consequences of such actions demean our spiritual occupation and positioning in the kingdom. The word of God warns that the world belongs to the devil, their father; who when he speaks, he tells lies, his native language and all that ooze out of his bowels are deceptions and there is no truth; as always, to be found inside of him. He steals the truth from the naive and unweaned individual, deceives the one that is not rooted in his faith and so steals his soul away.

I have good news that the lost can be found; the naive can gain understanding and deformed, lame man can receive strength again to walk and run with the congregation of the righteous. Have you been beaten, do you feel down and bruised? There is hope for the living. Help comes from above.

Jesus can restore you to the Father. Remember, even the lawful captive can be restored. He is able to save to the very end all those whose hearts are fixed on Him. Do you believe this?

1. **Fear of death, failure and success** (Hebrew 2:14-17)

The fear of death can kill a man before he really dies. The psyche of uncertainty beclouding a natural man on where he will end up on the other side of the divide creates a hollow in the heart. Since the devil knows that the fabrics of the soul are soft textured, especially when it is not woven with faith and confidence, he engages in puncturing the inner man (soul); beats it up with fear, uncertainty and doubt (FUD). He makes a man's heart float like bread on the water and begins to feed it with bad seed, the lies of the enemy. At the soul arena, the battle is won or lost; no wonder the scriptures declare:

"Keep your heart with all diligence for out of it flows the issues of life" Proverbs 4:23; and in another instructive construct it says; "we are not of them that draw back to perdition, but we are of them that believe to the saving of the soul" (Hebrew 10:37, 38). Fear has torment, and as it beats one's entire system up, the blood pressure begins to rise. You know the consequences of that. Some are constantly engaged in war with the enemy concerning death, failure and even success. People, who have for long, been subjected to the fear of death have suddenly reclining to drugs, tobacco and hyper reagents as a panacea. Fear can disorient a person's thinking and psyche;

and when mixed with doubt, drowns a man; resulting to a loss of self worth.

To checkmate this situation, one begins to ask oneself; "what is it that I fear most?" What sets my heart racing? At what point in the journey of life do I get hyper and unable to be the man in-charge of situations and circumstances? Does your heart jump at the mention of death? If this is the case, you need to make peace with God right away. Reach out to those who have offended you or who you have offended and begin a peace treaty now. Ask for forgiveness and restore relations today! The peace of God will gradually fill your heart again.

Invite the Lord of peace into your situation. Herod could not kill baby Jesus because God was in that project. Because the Lord made you for a specific purpose, He called you out to do a specific thing before He takes you to glory. Until you have completed your assignment, your time on Earth may not have been completed. The Lord made a way of escape for Joseph and Mary. He will make a way of escape for you. You were not saved to be disgraced in the streets. Your God will show Himself mighty on your stead.

Begin a prayer project that touches God's heart. Pray with fervency and unction. Pray with everything in you. Intercede, cry, wail and weep. You are in a war fare. IT IS A BATTLE FOR YOUR SOUL!

Get into the word of God fast. Study it to know the plan of God for your life. The heart deficient of the Word of God is a battle ground for war. The devil will suggest suicide, running away from home, drinking and every vice, just to get hold of your direction and your reasoning; to get hold of your soul. Deliver yourself from this insecure world and escape like a roe. You may be in the dark tunnel of life; all hope may seem lost and the enemy is almost winning in your game for life. Do not despair. God will send help. See, the world and all its fleeting shows will pass away, but he who does the will of God will abide forever. My friend Ron Walters wrote me a piece before I sent this script to the publisher, he said:

"Diocletian, the Roman Emperor, killed so many Christians and burned so many Bible manuscripts that he erected a column claiming Extincto Nomine Christianorum, meaning, 'The name of Christian is forever extinguished.'"

Voltaire, the famous French writer and atheist, in his most compelling argument, wrote, "Fifty years from now the world will hear no more of the Bible." Thomas Paine, to completely discredit the Bible, wrote in The Age of Reason, "When I get through, there will not be five Bibles left in America."

Albert Einstein, the man whom Time magazine named 'Man of the Century,' denied the existence of a personal God, but rather believed in pantheism.

Carl Sagan, the brilliant astrophysicist and Pulitzer Prize winner, said, "There is no God unless you call the Laws of Nature God."

Stephen Hawking, who achieved enormous scientific success despite suffering from severe ALS disease, said there is no heaven and there is no God, that it's "just a fairy tale for people who are afraid of the dark."

These people have won awards. They've written books. They're quoted in text books. They are listed in Wikipedia. The world recognizes their brilliance, but ... THEY'RE WRONG! They are the ones the Psalmist targeted when he wrote: "The One who rules in Heaven laughs out loud. The Lord scoffs at them." But on the other side we see Isaiah's words: "Those who hope in the Lord...will soar on wings like eagles ..." (Isaiah 40:31). Yes, they will! So, push back the doubt with faith. Cling to the word of God in this disbelieving culture ... and soar!"

2. He tricks men to hell with fancy, religious words

"Why do you not understand what I am saying? It is because you cannot hear My word. You are of your father the devil, and you want to do the desires of your father. He was a murderer from the beginning, and does not stand in the truth because there is no truth in him. Whenever he speaks a lie, he speaks from his own nature, for he is a liar and the father of lies." (John 8:43&44)

"He who overcomes will inherit these things, and I will be his God and he will be My son. But for the cowardly and unbelieving and abominable and murderers and immoral persons and sorcerers and idolaters and all liars, their part will be in the lake that burns with fire and brimstone, which is the second death." (Revelation 21: 7&8)

Herod told the wise men; **"go look for the baby and bring me words back when you have found him so that I may go to worship also."** That sounds like a godly man offering to go, worship. Not so with the devil. He is a high priest in religious affairs, crafting religious languages that soothe the aching soul, albeit, an un-weaned soul. In our age, here are some fancy religious, but devilish proposals or beliefs that are selling:

1. "Openness theology" which contends that God doesn't know what future choices people will make. It subjects God to a chance taker and thus tinkers on the truth of God's sovereignty.
2. Hell Fire is on Earth. This is a waning belief in an eternal hell, or human depravity. It is proposed that hell is what you experience on Earth; what your situation dictates; it believes that a good God cannot put people in hell, so there is no hell.

3. Sexual behavior is acceptable even outside of marriage. Those who hold such views argue that to make a wise choice, one must test the product to be sure that it right and good for the purpose of the purchase. So before they marry, they must 'try it out first'; "We are bed mates, nothing is wrong with it"

4. Heterosexuals or Homosexuals are the same. Lesbians or Gay should be given equal opportunity to lead the Church. It is politically acceptable. Permit me to say, "Even my dog would oppose this order and groan at the Church" (Read Roman 1: 18-25; Genesis 19).

5. The Scripture is NOT my authoritative Source for living. I will not allow God's Word to persuade me to believe what I do not like; what is contrary to what I have always believed and wanted to believe. The question should be asked; "do I believe it's even correct when it offends me?"

6. Open ended Theology: "you can have it all" worldview is a hodgepodge of biblical truth, undefined spirituality, and psychology; with twelve (12) step recoveries, and self-affirmations. The Open ended theology way is church-free; build-it-yourself spirituality that never condemns; speaks often of a higher power, sometimes God, sometimes Jesus.

7. Generic Spirituality: It asserts that all roads lead to heaven. Karma; Mohammed; Reincarnation? Buddhism, Hinduism, New Age, Angel-guided living. It's a "Have it your way" designer religion made to

order for a post-Christian culture. Just take note of the word of God. It states: **"Now the Bereans were of more noble character than the Thessalonians, for they received the message with great eagerness and examined the Scriptures every day to see if what Paul said was true"** (Acts 17:11).

8. Amorphous, shifting-faith that slides to the contours of individual preferences. This nurtures our tendency to self-edification, in which we strive to be our own gods, setting our own standards and controlling our own mini-universes. 'Do it my way' kind of thing.

9. Hydra headed path to God which suggests that: "the biggest mistakes humans make is to believe there is only one way." and adds that there are many diverse paths leading to what you call God." In the meantime, God says: **"Neither is there any other name under heaven given among men whereby we must be saved"** (Acts 4:12). Jesus remains the hub and center of all creation and path to God. There is no alternative path to seeking God.

10. "Truth is whatever you sincerely believe is true." "There's no such thing as truth." Is that a true statement? If so, then there is no such a thing as truth. So if the statement is true, it proves itself wrong. (Why does anyone go to college to learn truth from professors who believe there is no truth?). Jesus Christ is the TRUTH & the LIFE.

11. Moral Relativism: Church pew filled with All-inclusive doctrinal backlashes "come as you are, remain the way you came", "gather the tithes and offerings for our next project." This has no spiritual content towards heaven, or towards God. Moral relativism has no underlying substance to hold its structure or contend for what it believes is right. Relativism floats on the whims of what is socially and all inclusively prevailing. It has no substance or core values.

12. Freedom to live in sin because we are "Saved by grace, do anything under grace (including living in sin) and still be on our way to heaven." A woman preacher (Tele Evangelist) walked away from her marriage — without biblical grounds — because, in her words, "The Holy Spirit gave me peace about it"; she continues; "It is turning out for the glory of God and ministry is moving forward." She is still preaching and raising followers in the church, claiming the spiritual high ground. She says, "I've never been so close to God."

As religion creeps into Christianity we find such fancy words veiling the true meaning of "Christ-likeness" in us. Such fragrant and soothing echoes that lead men into error; believing that they are saved from the wrath of God with a form of godliness without a Savior who died on the cross and rose again; without a committed heart and surrendered will is sure to fan such men to hell. It was such a douse and coated practice displayed by proponents of the faith that led Karl Max to tell his followers that "religion is the opium of the people"; in other words; it is a tool to manipulate the psyche and intelligence of the naive and the ill-informed. We know the power in the gospel; that which changes a sinner to a saint; transforms a man from ordinary to a supernatural being; from a son of man to a son of God. The same power which raised Jesus up from the grave works heavily on all those who have had an encounter with Him. Such powers are not religious. They are supernatural spiritual powers and thus truths underlying them are transforming, potent and evidential in lives so claimed. These truths eat deep into the fabrics and cambiums of the bearer; they are not fancy religious words.

5.5 Jesus can deliver

As the world closes in on humanity, terrorism, hate crimes and barbarism make their home in the hearts of men, courtesy of demons and evil forces who represent Satan. Whether it is in politics or business or the civil society, Herod continues to show his presence in people, in politics and even on the pulpit. The assignment of Satan is clear: to kill, to steal and to destroy the precious seed of God in you.

5.5.1 Jesus is not a suggestion for life; he is the resurrection and the life

At the tomb of Lazarus, Jesus declared, I am the resurrection and the life. The true test of a man's worth, abilities and leadership is known at moments of controversy and seeming hopelessness. Jesus could have offered an easier way to the problem of Mary and Martha on the loss of their brother. One good answer would have been "he will rise on the resurrection with me" or "my peace be with you" or some other soothing words to pacify the ache and sorrow. No, it was time to declare Himself the Resurrection and the Life. Maybe in your home there is death that occurs at an underage and thus young men yield to the fear of death. It was for this reason Jesus came to this world. There is a fear that grips your heart at he mention of some Herod in your members; in your office. At such a time, your heart jumps and the fabrics of your being are eroded off their foundations. The fear of the unknown, fear of loss of job and many other fears continue to eat you up. Something has to be done about that experience. Jesus said; **"I am the resurrection and the Life."** Sometimes, God allows death and decay (so called) to happen so that He may show His glory. The essence is to showcase His glory. And that was what happened at Lazarus' tomb. As the Herods of our day declare war on innocent, defenseless children of the kingdom, the King of glory will be the shield and keeper of their souls. Jesus is the resurrection and the life. He will deliver completely, all those who trust in Him. Get up, cheer up, and the Lord will give you victory over the Herod in your life.

5.5.2 For the bruised, and emotionally wounded, he provides abundant and complete life

Mary looks tired from the labor room. She is recovering from the trauma and pain associated with child birth. Joseph is by her side with words of encouragement; he remembers the situation with the sheep and goats; the air posting a high-level ooze from the stench of the droppings. As they minced from the few cash to buy baby needs, it was obvious that the rough but joyful terrain of baby care has just begun. Joseph would have to increase his income or expand the carpentry business to make ends meet. The challenges that come with manhood starred at Joseph as Mary tried to recoup from the pain. She was excruciatingly exhausted and nothing should add to that trauma. As they waded through these new life and adjustments, the angel came with a message from God. **"Take the baby away, for Herod wants to kill him; run, go to Egypt."** Mary must have wondered what she got herself into. First it was a pregnancy without any relationship with a man; second the lipping of babies in the womb as she met Elizabeth; third the scorn and debate whether Joseph should put her away or not; third, prophecies to Joseph and

Mary around the birth of a Savior. As they wondered, wise men came to worship, gave gifts to this baby. And now Herod wants to kill the baby. There is so much happening at the same time. In Mary's little world, these are enough to traumatize the young girl. Joseph would look overwhelmed with all the incidences. It was nothing short of a state of confusion, hopelessness, and fatigue. What was meant to be a blessing seems to take a turn; a curse. But heaven has a different scheme and design for humanity through this 'trauma and fatigue' Have you been traumatized? Beaten and bruised so much that your observers can hardly recognize you? They say you are the architect of your misfortune; a wreck in time, having a hopeless eternity? God's word on you is final. Your creator has a plan and a purpose for your life. Your game is not over; truly, it has just begun. Your God is the presiding officer of the game. Here's what He says:

"The Lord is a jealous and avenging God;
the Lord takes vengeance and is filled with wrath.
The Lord takes vengeance on his foes
and vents his wrath against his enemies.
The Lord is slow to anger but great in power;
the Lord will not leave the guilty unpunished.
His way is in the whirlwind and the storm,
and clouds are the dust of his feet."
(Nahum 1:2&3 NIV)

You may have suffered abuse and neglect but God has a plan for your life. To such extent as there is life, a fragile, limping faith; just a stump in your frame, to that extent you begin to develop some spiritual muscles; you will not be broken. Mary was not broken. Joseph stood tall and faced his adversaries. Adversary and anguish come to test the stuff we are made of. The fabric of the soul is tested as the weather changes from 'cool and cozy' to some stormy, devastating moments of trial. The Herod in your life thinks you are undone, wasted, and a by-word. God calls you His beloved, precious in His sight. Decorated and prepared for great exploits. That's who you are. Remember, weeping may endue for a night, but joy comes in the morning. Your night is over. Truly, why God allowed you to experience this wilderness is that you may know that He is the Lord of all. He is an expert in gathering the pieces of our broken frames to mold new, but very important vessels of honor; so that no flesh will glory in His presence.

  At the face of death and hate, Mary and Joseph could have resorted to the blame game and self pity. They did not. Instead they listened to the word of life, to God who asked them to move to Egypt. Are you under an influence or certain disease has plagued your life all these years? Beaten and torn down? Get up, listen to your inner spirit as the Lord breathes on you His Spirit and you will see a direction towards Africa, a place of refuge. Seek the Lord while He may be found. This is your hour of deliverance, your moment to escape from your Herod and run to safety. The word of God declares, that affliction will not come to you the second time, you are free forever. Free and liberated in Jesus Christ. To run to safety, you must arise. You've got to do something. If you stay cold-footed, you will remain in your depraved state; you will always nurse your wounds and play the blame game. Get up, arise and locate help; run for your life! The story of the prodigal son in Luke 15: 11 through 32, teaches us to do something, even in the face of hopelessness:

"And when he came to himself, he said, How many hired servants of my father's have bread enough and to spare, and I perish with hunger! I will arise and go to my father, and will say unto him, Father, I have sinned against heaven, and before thee, And am no more worthy to be called thy son: make me as one of thy hired servants. And he arose, and came to his father. But when he was yet a great way off, his father saw him, and had compassion, and ran, and fell on his neck, and kissed him." (Luke 15:17-20 KJV)

I decree to you as you read this little book, that no enchantment or armory formed against you shall prosper. The enemy you see today, you will no more see and the Herod after your life will be met with heavenly forces, in the name of Jesus Christ. As much as you have decided to walk with the Lord and obey and serve Him all the days of your life, the Lord will defend you and uphold you in all your ways. The terror and fear of Herod; the annihilation of the wicked and inhumane treatment by mortals will be overridden by the Supernatural power in Christ Jesus. THS IS THE INHERITANCE OF THE CHILDREN OF THE MOST HIGH GOD. In quietness and in peace shall your strength be; your soul shall be preserved.

5.5.3 One solitary life

His world was aflame with excitements for their deliverance from shame and slavery; the government of the day waited in panic as to the personage of the King of the Jews. Behold after years of prophesies and expectations, He was born with more questions asked than their answers were provided.

He was a man born in an obscure village, the child of a peasant; yet inexperienced woman. His foster father was a carpenter; upcoming, eking out a living by subsistence means. He grew up in another village. He worked in a carpenter's shop until He was thirty, studiously inquiring and learning under the One who sent Him; and then for three years He was an itinerant preacher.

He never owned a home. He was made poor; the type that couldn't afford a meal for those who followed Him. He could not pay His taxes. He was objectionably, poor; poverty that was felt in the bones. When I inquired about this, I found that He chose the lifestyle on grounds of an expectation for those who would come later into His passage of times and embrace His life. He chose that life for the one reading this script.

He never wrote a book. He never went to formal school since the best His parents could afford was a Hebrew class for study of scriptures out of a scroll in the synagogue. His writings were His speeches to the elders and people of the temple and synagogue. As He spoke, some powers gripped His hearers and it was as if engrained on a marble. With some indelible ink His words echoes through the times and great writers have had the grace to remember and write much more than they had imagined. So this solitary life has produced many more books than those found in the world's libraries.

He never held an office. Yes, not a political office as the Jews were anticipating. On Earth He was a good for nothing kind of person on Wall Street or the London Fox Stock Exchange or the Malaysian Kuala Lumpur Market. Socially, He was an outcast that even the members of His family called Him names. Isaiah tells us that there was no form of beauty in Him at pseudo-trial that befell Him. His accusers and executioners ripped His body to shreds and beat Him beyond recognition. His flesh and blood littered the space. He never had a family. He never went to college. He never visited a big city nor lodged in a five star hotel. Judea of Galilee was all He knew and had His geography defined by the reach of fisher men's boat. Never owned a private jet or the sporty luxury cars of our day, yet His message travels more than the Air Force One. He did not travel more than two hundred miles from the place He was born and never did one of the things that usually accompany greatness. He had no credentials but Himself. He was simply a village boy, a community contradiction.

While still a young man, the tide of popular opinion turned against him. Because He was one of a kind- a legend radical whose opinion ran contrary to established order of the kingdom of Herod and Caesar and the Pharisees, He was seen as a rebel. His teachings were strong and persuasively convicting; His appeals were applauded by many who had not sold their souls to the evil that swept the land. Because He touched on the feeds and gains of the ruling order, their fear on loss of their livelihood generated to hatred and thus a vent of anger. They seized Him, to kill the innocent and the holy One. His friends ran away. One of them denied Him. He was turned over to His enemies. Enemies from the Temple where He had taught many; enemies who wore religious garbs and preached at Synagogues and Temples, including the High Priest whose job was to administer justice and equity and pray for the people. He went through the mockery of a trial. Beaten, rejected and tormented. He was nailed on a cross between two robbers with a six inch nail. While He was dying His executioners gambled for the only piece of property He had on earth – His coat. What a solitary life, a life no one would want to lead. As His last moments drew close, He prayed for His executioners and commended His soul to the Father. He drew His last breathe as a man and the Heavens, the Earth and the universe responded in one acclaim that King of Glory had completed His job on Earth; the Temple revolted and was ripped apart; the thunder responded in worship and the seas roared; signifying the majesty and glory of the King. He died, was laid in a borrowed grave through the pity of a friend and went in to the other world to deliver all those who were held captive and had all their life time been subjected to bondage. Jesus seized the keys of Hell and opened the gates of death. He devastated the Devil and freed his prisoners. Many were seen on the streets of Jerusalem after He arose; visibly walking around.

    Nineteen long centuries have come and gone, and today He is a centerpiece of the human race, the hub of history; the King of nations, beyond the Jews and leader of the column of progress. In Him all things consist and draw their lifeline. Without Jesus, nothing holds and nothing will ever hold. He remains a contradiction to those who defy the deity and supreme majesty of God. He is an offense to those who disbelieve and stay the course of evil.

Interesting He is coming back to Earth and all eyes will see Him. He comes to take away those who put their trust in Him and have had a share of His nature on Earth. He comes for a glorious Church filled with power and beauty; He comes for you if you have committed to serving and obeying His words of instruction from the Holy Writ. He comes, not for the preacher man or Bishop or some titled chiefs in the Temple whose occupation was filled with political tactics in ministry. He comes for the fellow on the street who has shunned evil and eschewed wickedness. He comes for the pastor who has a 'well done' dotting his engagement and ministrations; the one who looks up to God for help in ministry, who never contradicted the message of love and mercy with the judgment of God; who never preached with gains and worldly acquisitions in mind, running the course of Gehazi but chooses to serving, mentoring and sacrificing towards establishing a kingdom akin to heaven's.

Jesus was revealed to humanity to play the role of an advocate between a sinner and an angry God. His mission was to die for the sins of men that have offended God for years. Indeed, He died. He rose again from the grave, sealing forever the wall of offense and petitioned the Father on our behalf. As we speak, read, and run the course of this Earth, Jesus is interceding (making prayers for us). Jesus promises to take us home to heaven. Jesus will surely come to do that. Will you be home by then?

As He (Jesus) came in a crib, this time He comes as a King, the Messiah, the Governor of Nations. Will you be found in the family of God? Will you be in the convoy of the saints as the big supper treat lasts?

The times are winding up. The Lord Jesus will soon appear. Are you ready to receive Him? The Jews waited for a deliverer, God gave them a Savior. Nations today go for peace treaties; they come back with panaceas for temporary tranquilities. You have hoped in the help of man but until now, you received deceit and lies. Jesus comes as a King this time. He wants to reign with you, to establish a kingdom. I invite you into this Kingdom. As you bow in prayers, the Lord will fill you to over-flowing as He did to Mary.

Let us pray!

REFERENCES

Elendu, Emmanuel. "Unpublished Sermon Notes" Cincinnati; Dayton, OH: RCCG Dominion Center, 2002-2014.

Francis, James Allan. "Arise Sir Knight!" The Real Jesus and Other Sermons. Philadelphia: Judson Press, 1926. 123-124.

"Lifelines Publications" Unpublished Monthly Magazines. Cincinnati, OH: RCCG Dominion Center, 2010-2014.

Metzger, Bruce M. "A Lexicon of Christian Iconography" Church History, Vol. 45, No. 1 (Mar., 1976): 5-15.

Walters, Ron. "Pastor's Letter to Emmanuel Elendu" (2015)

"When God Drills a Man" Anonymous.

OTHER BOOKS BY EMMANUEL ELENDU

Commodity Map of Nigeria
Before You Quit
Digging for Gold
He Got Me Jazzed & Inspired

In the Press for 2017
Discipleship in the Digital Age

www.ingramcontent.com/pod-product-compliance
Lightning Source LLC
Chambersburg PA
CBHW070454100426
42743CB00010B/1615